MORE THAN WE ASKED OR
IMAGINED

MORE THAN WE ASKED OR
IMAGINED

THE SPIRITUAL JOURNEY
OF A SIXTY-YEAR CANCER SURVIVOR

STEVE POLL
WITH BETH POLL

More Than We Asked or Imagined
Copyright © 2022 by Steve and Beth Poll

Published by Steven M. Poll
Grand Rapids, Michigan

All rights reserved. No part of this publication may be reproduced, stored in a retrieval system, or transmitted in any form or by any means—for example, electronic, photocopy, recording—without the prior written permission of the publisher. The only exception is brief quotations in printed reviews.

Scriptures marked ASV are taken from the *American Standard Version*, public domain.

Scriptures marked NKJV are taken from the *New King James Version*®. Copyright© 1982 by Thomas Nelson, Inc. Used by permission. All rights reserved.

Scriptures marked NIV are taken from The Holy Bible, *New International Version*®, *NIV*®. Copyright© 1973, 1978, 1984, 2011 by Biblica, Inc.® Used by permission of Zondervan. All rights reserved worldwide.

Scriptures marked KJV are taken from *The Holy Bible, King James Version*, public domain.

This publication is intended to provide helpful and informative material on the subjects addressed. The information given in *More Than We Asked or Imagined* is biblical and spiritual in nature. It is not professional counsel and should not be viewed as such. The medical information presented has also been set in its corresponding historical time frame. Readers should consult their personal health professionals before adopting any of the suggestions in this book or drawing inferences from it. The authors and publisher/printer specifically disclaim all responsibility for any liability, loss or risk, personal or otherwise, that is incurred as a consequence, directly or indirectly, of the use of and/or application of any contents of this book.

Note also that the names and details of individuals in some of the testimonies and stories have been altered to protect their privacy.

Front cover main photograph: NRX Nuclear Reactor Courtesy of Toronto Public Library.
Front cover additional photographs: Winnifred Poll
Back cover photograph: Steve Poll
Interior photography: Unless otherwise indicated, provided by the Poll family

Cover designed: Jeanette Gillespie
Interior designed: Beth Shagene

Publisher's Cataloging-in-Publication Data

Names: Poll, Steve, author. | Poll, Beth, author.
Title: More than we asked or imagined : the spiritual journey of a sixty-year cancer survivor / Steve and Beth Poll.
Description: [Grand Rapids, Michigan] : Steven M. Poll, [2022]
Identifiers: ISBN: 979-8-9854723-0-1 (trade paper)
Subjects: LCSH: Cancer in children—Patients—United States—Biography. | Cancer—Patients—United States—Biography. | Cancer—Treatment—Technological innovations—Canada. | Cobalt Isotopes—Therapeutic use. | Cancer—Treatment—Complications. | Spiritual healing. | Miracles. | Christian biography. | Christian life. | God (Christianity)—Love. | Cancer patients' writings, American. | BISAC: MEDICAL / Oncology / Pediatric. | RELIGION / Faith. | RELIGION / Christian Living / Inspirational.
Classification: LCC: RC265.6.P65 P65 2022 | DDC: 362.196994/0092—dc23

Printed in the United States of America

This story is dedicated to three groups of people:

First, in memory of the children who were diagnosed with the same type of cancer as I was and did not survive.

Second, to the various scientists who were involved in the development of the powerful technology used in my treatment, and to the medical staff mentioned in this book, who were willing to risk using this technology as a last option on a newborn in the midst of a life-and-death struggle.

Finally, but most importantly, to the named and unnamed people mentioned in this book. In various ways, you have all played a role in my coming to realize that Jesus was always there for me, and was doing more for my family and me than we could ever have asked or imagined.

Contents

1. Not Expected to Live...9
2. 3,500 Rads...20
3. Enjoying the Early Years..29
4. Another Unique Challenge 38
5. Still in the Mainstream 44
6. High School's Ups and Downs...............................53
7. Building Roads and Romance 63
8. Grim Tales and a Fairy Tale 78
9. Blazing Trails as Newlyweds 88
10. Reaching Out..97
11. Filtered Theology and Starting a Family 113
12. The Downward Spiral..124
13. Spiritual Showdowns, Heavenly Healings 139
14. The Testimony Travels 155
15. For Us and for Our Children 161
16. New Teachings, New Habits..................................165
17. God Is God, and We Are Not.................................171
18. Having an Influence on Our World 179
19. He Was There All the Time 186
20. The Teardrop Trailer Testimonies..........................193
21. At the Point of Our Need 205
22. Followed by Goodness and Mercy 214

Acknowledgments 227
About the Authors 228

1

Not Expected to Live

There is a small white church on the corner of Hanna Lake Avenue and 68th Street in Dutton, Michigan. In the fall of 1960, there was much anticipation in the congregation that met in that building because five couples were expecting a child. My parents were especially excited. I was to be their firstborn. Most of their friends who married about the same time they did already had children. Dad had an army buddy who lived several miles away. His wife was expecting their third child. Every one of these pregnancies was going well, with no signs of trouble. All five babies from the church were born in a ten-day period in late October. I was one of these children. As was the custom, when more than one baby was born in a short time frame, one baptism service would be held, and all the newborns would be baptized at one time. Four babies were baptized in mid-November. I was not one of them. Things did not go as expected for me.

Early on the afternoon of October 16, my mother started having contractions. When she called the doctor, she was told not to go to the hospital until the contractions were regularly spaced and a matter of minutes apart. Throughout the night, contractions were variable and quite strong. In the morning, she was advised to go into the hospital.

After the initial excitement of grabbing the suitcase, driving to Butterworth Hospital in Grand Rapids, and getting Mom checked in, my dad was escorted to the labor room where he was allowed to see my mother for a few minutes. After that, he was directed to the fathers' waiting room, as was the practice at the time. There was a big clock on the wall of the waiting room. During the first couple of hours, Dad spent his time glancing at the clock and wondering how things were going, as well as feeling the anticipation of being a father. After a few hours passed, he began to see other men who had arrived at the waiting room after him being congratulated on a birth and being escorted to see their wives. Wondering gave way to concern. Dad began to pace the floor. A couple of times during the afternoon and evening, he was allowed to make the long walk back to the labor room to see Mom. He was informed that the birth process was not progressing normally. From time to time he would get an update: "Your wife is still in labor." Nighttime came, and he slept in a chair in the waiting room. When he awoke the news was the same: "Your wife is still in labor."

Now it was the morning of October 18. Mom had been in labor for over forty hours. The situation was beginning to look impossible. Mom had learned years before to give what looked like impossible physical situations to God. When she was nine years old she had appendicitis. Her appendix burst and she became unconscious. This was in 1943, during the Second World War, and penicillin was not yet available. The doctors told her parents nothing could be done. My grandfather told the doctors, "You can't just let her die. You have to do something!"

The doctors performed emergency surgery to install drains that would drain out the infectious fluid. She remained unconscious for six weeks. Her mother stayed at the hospital with her for the first three of those.

My mother's parents had started to grow in their faith and had joined a church a few years before this happened. They were learning to give their cares to God. They spent quite a bit of time on their knees praying for her. In the small rural community she grew up in, people were deeply concerned for neighbors. The church members were praying too. The pastor made frequent visits to the house to see my grandparents, and to the hospital to see their little girl.

It was twenty miles from the farm to the hospital, not far by today's standards. In 1943 there were war restrictions, however, and car tires were being rationed. The sixteen-year-old Model T Ford my grandparents owned rarely made a round trip to the hospital without needing an inner tube patched or having a minor breakdown.

After Mom regained consciousness, she told God that if she recovered, she would be a good wife and mother when she grew up. She spent eight more weeks in the hospital. After an extended recuperation time, doctors performed a second surgery. She spent a lot of time in bed, working things out between herself and God while she went through the whole ordeal. That year, she attended her one-room school the first week in the fall and the last week in the spring.

Labor Room Test of Faith

Now as an adult in a difficult medical scenario, Mom was told the birth process was too far along to attempt a C-section. In the labor room she was having her faith tested again, but she held on.

For Dad, trying to read magazine articles only did so much to take his mind off the situation. He continued to pace back and forth while the passing time was marked by the hour hand on the clock moving from one hour to the next.

The hospital staff was giving Mom excellent care. One nurse in particular went above and beyond to do what she could. She was a short, energetic lady, and she would climb up on the hospital bed so she could get the leverage to move Mom into a different position. One of the hospital staff suggested to Dad that he go home to get a good nap and a change of clothes, but he would not leave.

A few times that day, Dad was allowed back in the labor room for a brief visit. The updates continued to be the same: "Your wife is still in labor." Evening came again, and with it another night in the waiting room. The next morning, the update was the same. Another long day of pacing. Another day of the clock slowly moving from one hour to the next.

Meanwhile, in the labor room the obstetrician told my mother, "When labor has gone this long without progressing further, there are complications and one of the two of you is not going to make it."

Yet Mom had seen God bring her through what appeared to be an insurmountable physical challenge in the past. She did not allow that statement to shake her faith.

Finally, after seventy-four hours of labor, I was born a little before 4:00 p.m. on October 19.

Dad had worn out the soles of his shoes.

Something Wasn't Right . . .

As soon as I was born, the medical people in the delivery room knew something was not right. I was not breathing, and the usual slap on the bottom was not enough. I had passed meconium before I was born, and during the labor process I had gotten that material into my lungs. Mom got just a glimpse of me before the delivery team rushed into action, attempting to get me to breathe. There was concern that I could have brain damage due to lack of oxygen. The team was not sure they would be successful. It was a long time before I was breathing properly. Later, the doctors told my mother that they believed I had experienced such low oxygen levels near the end of the birthing process that I had attempted to breathe on my own before I was actually born!

After my breathing stabilized, I was put into an incubator in the regular nursery. My newborn picture was taken. My parents were able to get a good look at me at that time. My abdomen was black and blue due to the trauma of the extended labor. They were hopeful that the trauma was past and that I would be able to go home soon.

Dad finally decided it would be a good time to go home and get some real sleep. After he woke up and took a shower, he went to the kitchen to call his army buddy and tell him he had a son. While he was dialing the rotary phone, he heard a knock on the door. His army buddy had been trying to call dad and had kept getting no answer, so he drove over to tell him his wife had given birth to a son at another hospital. We both were born on the same day.

Within hours, it was discovered that I could not keep the feedings of baby formula in my system. I was transferred to what was known as the sick baby nursery, where I remained in an incubator. There, a procedure called an intravenous cutdown was performed to attach IV tubing to my ankles. This tubing was used to administer fluids to keep me hydrated and to administer medications if needed. These small incisions were located just above the ankle bone on the inner sides of both ankles. I have the scars from this procedure to this day. Due to my growth, the scar lines are now about an inch long and two inches above my ankle bones.

If you walk through an older cemetery, you may notice a grave marker that simply states *Baby*. Years ago, newborns were not legally named right away, so those who were sickly and passed away in the first few days of life were not given a name. When I showed no signs of improvement, my parents were told not to name me. I was expected to live no more than three days.

Three days passed and I was still alive, but I was steadily losing weight. Another day passed, and then another. I remained under close observation in the sick baby nursery. My birthweight was eight pounds, two ounces. By the end of my first week, I had dropped to six pounds, two ounces. I had lost 24 percent of my body weight.

My mother was discharged from the hospital the morning of my eighth day. She returned to the hospital that evening to feed me and take care of me. When she was changing my diaper that evening, she noticed a strange tint in the color of my urine. It looked like the orange Hi-C drink. She was alarmed and told the nurse's aide something was wrong. The aide told her that having a tint in the urine one time was nothing to be concerned about. Mom then went to the charge nurse and got the same response. But Mom could be very persistent. She kept pushing the issue and went through both the intern and resident, getting the same type of response. She told them, "I did my pediatric rotation in nursing school, and this color urine is not normal." Finally, around 1:00 a.m., the staff called Dr. Donald Johns, who would become my pediatrician. He arrived at the hospital at 2:00 a.m.

The Wilms Tumor

Dr. Johns examined me. He knew the tint in the urine was a potential sign of a Wilms tumor. Wilms is a cancer of the kidney typically affecting young children, with approximately five hundred cases reported in the United States each year. In seven percent of Wilms tumors detected, blood spilling into the urine is the first sign leading to detection. Only one time did I have this discolored urine. In the days before ultrasounds and CT scans, the way to confirm a Wilms was to palpate the abdomen. Most Wilms tumors are a single mass on either the left or right side. If a tumor was found during the palpation, the location and an estimate of size could be determined.

This activity was risky, but there was really no option. In a 1959 speech given by C. Evert Koop, who later became the United States Surgeon General, he warned medical teams not to have multiple people palpating a Wilms. This was due to the fact that these tumors typically were essentially loose inside and were surrounded by a capsule that could rupture and metastasize. Dr. Johns went ahead and palpated my black-and-blue abdomen as carefully as he could, and sure enough, he felt a mass in my left side.

In 1960, the only way to really determine the nature and extent of a Wilms was to do an exploratory surgery with the intent of completely removing the tumor, if possible. The actual state of the cancer tumor in a Wilms patient can vary considerably from one patient to another, so the outcome of surgery could not be predicted in advance.

A consultation meeting was held concerning my case. Dr. Johns met with Dr. Dewey, who was appointed chief of surgery about the time I was born, and Dr. Meeuwsen, a urologist who was a veteran of the U.S. Army, where he served as a surgeon with the 97th Infantry Division in both Germany and Japan during World War II.

With my weight steadily dropping, a decision had to be made. Doing surgery on an infant in my condition would be risky, but not doing anything would make it just a matter of time until I was unable to survive. The consensus was to schedule emergency surgery for the next day, day ten of my life. The plan was that Dr. Meeuwsen would be the primary surgeon, and Dr. Dewey would be present to act as a consultant so my condition could be analyzed by a second expert as the surgery progressed. I was to be the smallest patient either of these surgeons had ever operated on.

Another issue was that pain medication appropriate for use with an infant was unavailable in Grand Rapids at the time. It was simply too costly to keep on hand. As soon as the consultation between my doctor and the surgeons was over, arrangements had to be made to have a medication supplier in Chicago prepare an expensive formulation and put it on an overnight flight to Grand Rapids so it would be available in time for my surgery the next morning!

Despite the recommendation not to name me, Mom and Dad had insisted that my name be on record. They were at the hospital when an identification band was put on my wrist just before surgery. The band had a little puppy printed on it, with *Steven Michael Poll 10 Days Old* handwritten behind the puppy. I was taken out of the bassinet, along with the various types of medical tubing I was attached to, and placed in the middle of an adult-sized gurney. Then I was wheeled off to surgery. As I left, Mom and Dad got on their knees next to the big green chairs in the waiting room and gave me back to God.

When the operating team opened me up, they found the upper two-thirds of my left kidney had developed improperly and was a cancerous mass that had intertwined with my intestine and extended over to the edge of the right kidney. The mass was considered a loose tumor and inoperable the way they found it. Any removal attempt would likely cause a metastasis. They also found that the tumor had tiny fingers extending into the surrounding tissue. This would prevent complete removal, and the tumor would continue to grow if the larger portion were removed.

After the surgery, my parents were told nothing more could be done for me. They were also told that the surgery had been very taxing on my body. Once again, they were told I could not be expected to live more than three days.

Making Things Happen

Dad's early life experiences shaped his response to the doctors. He was raised as if he were an only child, because his brother was grown and out of the house by the time Dad started school. His father passed away the day before my dad turned sixteen. The previous fall, Dad managed taking in the crops on the farm himself. In high school, he played football. The coach was a no-nonsense kind of person. So was the assistant coach. Dad told a story about the assistant coach bailing out of a B-17 bomber during World War II and returning on his own through enemy lines. These men had instilled in the team that they were to be dedicated to the cause and were responsible to make things happen. If a starter had a bad couple of plays, the coach would take him out for a quarter, to show him he could be replaced. Each player had to consistently get the job done when he was given the responsibility. The coach used to tell them frequently, "There is no reason you should ever let anyone score a point."

Dad had learned his lessons well. He was co-captain of the team his senior year, and they outscored their competition that season 234 to 0. He still knew how to make things happen. When I was alive after three days, he told the doctors, "You have to do something—I don't care what it costs!"

So, what were the doctors to do? They had a sickly newborn on their hands with a diagnosed stage III cancerous kidney. This baby was recovering from major abdominal surgery, with an open incision almost halfway around his body. Most children diagnosed with a Wilms were diagnosed at around thirty-six months of age and did not usually have complications prior to treatment, beyond the Wilms itself. The doctors told my parents the five-year survival rate for stage III Wilms patients in relatively good condition was under 10 percent. Beyond that, chemotherapy coming on the scene as the choice of treatment for Wilms was still a few years away.

Consultation meetings between my doctors became a daily event. Before anything could be done, they felt that I needed to stabilize after the surgery. With Dad pushing them to take some action, they even considered simply scheduling a second surgery when I stabilized.

A broader consultation meeting was held. Once again, Dr. Johns met with Dr. Dewey and Dr. Meeuwsen. Joining them this time was Dr. Wahby, the chief radiologist on staff at the hospital. It was determined that the only remotely practical medical possibility to prepare me for a successful second surgery involved developing a plan to use the Theratron unit the hospital had purchased a few years earlier.

The Theratron Plan

This Theratron machine had its roots in 1940s nuclear research. During World War II, the materials used in atomic research in Europe were moved from France to England to keep them out of the hands of the Nazis. When England was threatened, these materials were moved to Canada, where a nuclear research facility was constructed. In the mid-1940s, this research facility designed and built an experimental nuclear reactor called the NRX, which was put into service in 1947. In the decade after the war, the power of this reactor was increased to the point that it had ten times more neutron flux than any other reactor in the entire world.

When operating at this level, the NRX was the only reactor in the world that was powerful enough to be used to create man-made cobalt 60—a radioactive isotope—in a form that could be used effectively in treating deep-seated tumors. Cobalt 60 can give off gamma radiation at different rates, depending on how quickly it receives radiation from neutron bombardment when formed in a reactor. Only the NRX had enough neutron flux at the time to convert inactive cobalt 59 into a highly radioactive form of cobalt 60 that would emit enough gamma ray intensity to be used medically in this way. The process of the NRX creating this type of cobalt 60 isotope was not fast at all, however. It involved putting ordinary cobalt metal in rods, placing the rods in the reactor, and leaving them exposed to the neutron flow for up to a year and a half.

When put into service in 1956, the hospital's Theratron machine contained cobalt 60 created in the NRX reactor. This machine was manufactured by an organization named Atomic Energy of Canada Limited. The Canadian government had created this organization with a directive to develop peaceful applications of nuclear technology. The Theratron was classified as a mega-voltage machine producing the same effect as a two-to-three-million-volt X-ray. The radiation would have the effect of shrinking and consolidating the tumor so it could be removed surgically.

Dr. Wahby was in charge of the radiology unit at the hospital. He had studied medicine in Canada's city of London, at the University of Western Ontario in the early 1950s. At that time, the cobalt 60 radiation technology was just being developed and becoming commercially available. His internship was at Victoria Hospital in London, Ontario, the first hospital to use a cobalt 60 unit on a patient. That first patient was treated on October 27, 1951. Dr. Wahby also spent a year studying at the New England Medical Center in Boston. He had never used the Theratron on a newborn before. A newborn posed a new set of challenges since the tumor was a very small target, and uncomfortable newborns do not lie still upon request. It was unknown if a newborn could survive the effects of the radiation, especially a newborn in my condition.

Dr. Wahby had been gaining experience with the Theratron unit since it had been installed in 1956. From what he told my parents, it appears that a month before I was born the hospital had received a new, more powerful radiation source for the Theratron. This would cut in half the amount of time required at each treatment session. (Cobalt 60 has a half-life of just over five years, so the original radiation source had lost about half of its radioactivity since it had been installed.) The immediate concern was, would I be able to survive the cobalt treatments?

In 1952 the Canadian magazine *Maclean's* featured an article on one of the first cobalt machines to be used. The article by Eric Hutton was entitled "The Atom Bomb That Saves Lives." The article referred to the cobalt 60 radiation source as a *Cobalt Bomb*. The choice of this nickname for the new technology was influenced by the fact that just six years earlier, the atomic bombs were used in Japan. The intent of the *Cobalt Bomb* involved a peaceful use of radiation—to bombard tumor cells using gamma rays. Cobalt in the form used in the treatment machine was not explosive, but according to the article, the half-inch-thick stack of cobalt disks the size of a quarter was releasing radiation at a rate so fast that that six hundred billion gamma rays would reach the patient each minute. The *Maclean's* article described the goal of planning and executing cobalt therapy by featuring the following discussion between a medical student and his professor:

> Grasping the theory of radiation, the student said brightly: "Oh, it's like finding a man in the coils of a boa constrictor. You take careful aim, hoping to hit the snake and not the man."
>
> "No," answered the professor drily, "you hope to put more bullets into the snake than into the man."[1]

Mom was working for a family doctor just before I was born. He was well informed concerning the challenges surrounding radiation therapy. He was of the opinion that an infant in my condition would not survive the radiation. Nonetheless, the consensus of the doctors at the hospital was to develop a Theratron treatment plan and proceed when it was decided that I had recovered sufficiently from surgery to undergo treatment. My situation was monitored closely because the tumor itself was an ever-increasing threat.

---

1. Eric Hutton, "The Atom Bomb That Saves Lives," *Maclean's*, February 15, 1952, accessible at https://archive.macleans.ca/article/1952/2/15/the-atom-bomb-that-saves-lives.

2

3,500 Rads

While I was recovering from surgery, bills were adding up for my parents. At that time, newborns were not covered by insurance if they had not left the hospital after thirty days. Since Mom was a nurse and had been doing a good job taking care of me at the hospital, the medical staff felt she would be able to take care of me at home. Plans were made for my release.

Mom's early life experiences had prepared her well for taking care of me. After her hospitalization as a child, she wanted to become a nurse. She grew up on a small farm near McBain, Michigan. Soon after she graduated from high school, an opportunity to pursue her dream presented itself. One Sunday evening after the young people's society meeting at church, a couple of other recent graduates announced that they were leaving in the morning for Grand Rapids. They had friends who had done the same and had gotten jobs in a car part plating factory. It seems the main qualification was, "If you are from up north and have manure on your shoes, you're hired."

Even in the city, farm kids had a reputation for being able to work. Mom had put in many hours picking beans on the farm and was known as the champion bean picker in her community. She also had started driving her uncle's Oliver tractor when she was nine. Mom got home late that night after the meeting, packed her bag, told her parents what she was doing, and left early in the morning. On arrival, she went into the office of the plating company in Grand Rapids and told them she was looking for a job. The manager asked her, "Where are you from?" When she answered McBain, he motioned toward the interior of the plant and said, "Go on back and get started."

Mom worked at the factory for several months to save money ahead for nursing school. While in nursing school, she worked as a waitress to pay room and board. Money was tight. She once said she was given a leftover orange from the restaurant and put off eating it in case she needed it later. She waited so long that it dried up. Her nursing school was old-school, and her instructors were veteran army nurses. White shoes always had to be perfectly polished. Preparing patients' food was meticulous. You even had to peel an orange a certain way so that you had only one piece of peel when you were finished. Everything was done by the book, and there was no room for errors. Yet Mom met every challenge. The date on Mom's first nursing license is five years to the day before I was born.

Eggnog and Old Crow

After my surgery, Mom asked Dr. Johns for suggestions on caring for my open incision. In the days before plastic wound dressings, it was difficult to keep dressings dry. It was not that she was unfamiliar with dressings. She had been a surgical nurse the first few years after she had graduated from nursing school. Dr. Johns told her that she had been doing fine caring for her baby and to "take him home and love him." He was of the opinion that even though I was given excellent care in the hospital, I would do even better at home. So home I went, with an open incision in my black-and-blue abdomen.

I was too weak to suck on a bottle properly, but Mom had a plan to get me to gain weight. With the doctor's approval, she cut two small slits in an X shape on the end of the bottle nipple and put eggnog in my evening bottle. I was still having problems keeping food down, but after she did that my weight started to stabilize. In an effort to avoid the high cost of pain medication, Dr. Johns had also suggested that she administer a precise amount of whiskey drops to me. He said it would have the same effect on me as the pain medication from Chicago. A bottle of Old Crow was obtained.

It was not Mom's first time caring for a child with a Wilms tumor. When she was in nursing school there was a five-year-old patient at the hospital who had a history of Wilms. This girl had wonderful parents, and many stuffed animals kept her company in her hospital room. She had been diagnosed when she was three and had a tumor removed from one side, and the wound had healed. Two years later, a remnant of the tumor had grown and was affecting her remaining kidney. There was nothing the doctors could do for her. Mom recalled that the girl experienced quite a bit of discomfort with her distended abdomen from the tumor. After her nursing shift, Mom would punch out and go read books to this young girl. Before long, the girl passed away.

Despite watching this young patient pass away, Mom had faith that I would make it. Just after my surgery, when my short-term survival was in question, a card from a photography studio came in the mail. The studio was offering a package that included several sessions of baby and toddler photographs. In addition, the studio was a marketing arm for a baby furniture company. Mom called the studio and arranged for a sales representative to come to the house. After the rep's presentation, she and Dad decided to spend $300 on a package that included the series of photographs, a "modern" playpen, and a Baby Butler—a highchair that would convert into an activity table and a swing as a child grew. I was still too young to use either of these pieces of baby furniture, even if I were healthy, but purchasing them was an act of faith on my parents' part. Mom then purchased a dresser full of baby clothes. One of the neighbor ladies told me years later that as Mom went through the whole ordeal, she showed her what having a trusting faith in God was. This neighbor said she had never seen such faith.

I was to be home for Thanksgiving. Even though each day was a challenge, it was a dream come true for my parents. Mom would place me on a pillow and wrap a blanket around me and the pillow together. That created a bundle so Dad could hold me without disturbing my open incision. One of the neighbors lent my parents a small one-year crib on wheels so I could be wheeled from one room to another, and so we could have a few quiet moments in the living room as a family between feedings. My ability to keep a significant amount of food down had not improved, so the time between feedings was not very long. My parents enjoyed Thanksgiving dinner around their little table in the kitchen, with me in the little crib nearby. They offered prayers of thanks because their baby was home. When I was baptized on the Sunday of Thanksgiving weekend, I wore a newborn-size romper for the service.

The "Radiation Bunker"

The doctors decided I had recovered enough from surgery to start cobalt treatments the week after Thanksgiving. That Monday, Mom put me in her blue-and-white 1956 Ford and drove me down a few country roads and then down some city streets, to the hospital. She kept a spit cloth nearby to wipe up my projectile vomiting along the way.

After we arrived at the hospital, I was taken to the "radiation bunker" to be prepped for the first cobalt 60 treatment. This was a specially constructed underground room that housed the cobalt radiation machine. The walls of the bunker were four feet thick. They were constructed of dense concrete lined with lead blocks to prevent harmful levels of radiation from reaching the outside.

The radiation machine itself was a large unit with a heavy base on one end. In the center, attached to the base, was a large, upright, C-shaped arm that could tilt from side to side. One end of the arm had a 4,000-pound lead weight mounted on it to counterbalance the radiation head, a heavy lead-and-tungsten structure containing the radioactive cobalt 60 on the other end of the arm. The patients would typically lie on the table with the radiation head over them and the counterweight under them. The lead in the counterweight absorbed most of the transmitted radiation after it passed through the patient. To change the angle of the radiation beam, the whole arm could rotate around the patient lying on the table. The rotation function was used in most adult treatments because it would overlap the moving beam on the tumor at all times and minimize the exposure of surrounding tissues.

The radiation head had a small-diameter tube that could be attached to it, which contained a measuring tape. This tube served as a pointer to pinpoint where on the body the radiation would enter, and the tape was used to determine the proper distance from the radiation source to the point inside the body intended to receive the calibrated dosage of radiation. The treatment table would be adjusted to the proper height based on the measurement. The tube and measuring tape would be removed when the machine was in use.

The hospital employed a medical physicist who had been thoroughly trained to measure the output of the radiation source and adjust the exposure time to ensure each patient received a proper dosage. This adjustment was necessary to take into account the constant decay of the radiation source. The physicist would also determine the depth and angle of a treatment, based on the size of the patient and the prescription dose set by the radiologist. The goal of using the Theratron was to kill and/or shrink a tumor effectively while minimizing damage to surrounding healthy tissue.

Due to my size, the treatment program that Dr. Wahby designed for me called for operating the Theratron in a stationary mode, using what was called a "wedged pair" technique. This technique required me to receive radiation from one direction while lying on my back, and then be repositioned on my side, with the radiation source remaining stationary so I could receive radiation from the other perpendicular direction. The result would be that I would receive radiation from two directions at a 90 degree angle to each other. To ensure that the tumor received uniform radiation but the surrounding tissue had minimal exposure, the width of the radiation beam would be set as prescribed to match the width of the tumor. In addition, for both exposures a lead wedge was to be placed in the path of the beam to reduce the intensity at one side of the beam. When the effect of the two beams would overlap, a tailor-made rectangular region of uniform radiation dose would be produced in my body.

In theory, this planned process would be quite straightforward.

The staff operating the unit would position me on my back, set the width of the beam, place the wedge, and activate the Theratron. After exposing me to the beam while on my back, the staff would reposition me on my side, the beam width would be changed, the lead wedge repositioned, and I would be exposed again. The end result would direct radiation to concentrate uniformly in a "shoebox" target area containing the tumor.

The plan was to administer a total of 100 rads of radiation at each treatment appointment. My actual exposure time to achieve this would be less than five minutes.

Sandbagged . . .

One of the first things the staff operating the unit did to prepare me for my treatment was to mark out the radiation targets on my body. They used a permanent marker to plot out the targets on my skin. I was then positioned on the table in the treatment room. Sandbags were placed on the table behind me to keep me in place during the radiation exposure.

Despite all of their careful preparations, a baby who cannot keep food down and feels discomfort from major surgery does not lie still. The staff would get me properly positioned against the sandbags and then leave me and go into the control room, which had thick lead walls to protect them from radiation. They would start the treatment and watch me through a small, thick window of leaded glass. The radiation itself was painless, but due to my condition I typically would start crying and moving by the time the treatment would begin, or soon after. They would then have to stop the treatment and reposition me. Their attempt to solve the problem of my moving was to tie me to the sandbags so I could not move. Yet even tied to the sandbags, I could still wiggle enough to shift the target. That happened frequently. Ensuring that the radiation was not directed to the wrong area when I shifted required the constant attention of the staff as they watched me through the window of the control booth. It also required a lot of patience.

Day after day, Mom would bundle me up and brave the weather to bring me to the hospital. On the drive in, she would be praying for me. Every day I would either have issues with projectile vomiting or be intermittently crying from pain. At each visit, the staff would take me from her and put me in my bassinet to check me over. I say "my" bassinet because it had my name on it and a sign that read *Do not wash*. The staff did not want anyone to wash the radiation target markings off me. After the daily examination, I would be placed on the table and be tied to the sandbags. Then I would be left alone under the large structure containing the radiation source as the staff moved into the control booth and started the process once again.

During the weeks involving my treatments, one Sunday after the morning service at church a deacon approached my dad as he was getting into his car. The deacon asked him if the family needed help with medical bills. Dad's response was, "As long as I have a job, we'll be all right."

Thirty-five times Mom brought me to the hospital for the radiation treatments. After seven weeks, my treatments were over. By mid-January 1961, I had received a total of 3,500 rads of radiation. To put this in perspective, depending on the circumstances the radiation exposure *limit* for a nuclear industry worker is the equivalent of two to five rads a year.

At the end of the treatment time, I still was not keeping nourishment down the way I should. Mom was continuing with her eggnog feeding plan, so I was growing and my weight was going up slightly. But during the weeks of radiation treatments, my legs had gotten so thin that the only way to keep my socks on was to secure them with rubber bands around my ankles.

The plan post-radiation had been to do a second surgery to remove the tumor and the remnant of the associated kidney as soon as the cobalt treatments were completed. This second surgery was postponed a little to give me time to gain strength. Ten days after the last cobalt 60 treatment, however, my parents brought me back to the hospital for surgery. Once again, they gave me to God as I went into the operating room.

When Dr. Meeuwsen and the operating team opened me up this time, they found that the tumor had shrunk and had been consolidated, as Dr. Wahby predicted. What was unexpected was the discovery that the tumor contained hair and teeth. Over the years, many theories have been put forth on the cause of a Wilms tumor. When tumor tissues have been studied from different patients, different types of tissues have been found. Cases like mine led the doctors to a theory that Wilms, at least at times, resulted from an identical twin being developed but without forming properly.

Approaching Normal!

After the surgery, I stayed in the hospital for observation and recovery for a week. Once again, it was soon decided that I would be better off recovering at home. It would be a ten-day wait after the surgery, however, before the pathology report would come back—ten days of my parents going to God with their concerns. Then the report came back with the statement, "No surrounding live cells." The medical intervention efforts to defeat the tumor had been successful!

Still, some concerns remained. After the second surgery, I was still not taking nourishment as I should. In photos taken just after my second operation, my appearance was very gaunt. I suppose the way I looked was to be expected. I looked like a scaled down version of an adult who had just gone through an extended period of minimal nutrition and maximum medical trauma.

Every week, I was taken to Dr. Johns' office for observation and to be weighed. Eventually, I started gaining as much as a pound a week. Dr. Johns would tell my mother, "You're a good mom!" I weighed seventeen pounds, eight ounces at my six-month checkup. This put me very close to the normal weight for a healthy developing baby boy at that age. The rapid weight gain was remarkable. Dr. Johns was of the opinion that my basic survival was due to divine intervention, and he also attributed my weight gain after the radiation and surgery trauma had passed to the same power of God.

The long and deep incision line around the left side of my waist and abdomen was still open, but it was healing. Mom continued diligently with dressing changes. Our house had a south-facing picture window in the living room, and she would place me in front of this window so the late winter sunlight could shine on the incision. By the time I was seven months old, the incision had closed up and the skin was healed over.

In my six-month studio photo, I am a chubby baby with a full head of hair. Looking at the photograph, you would never know I had any history of health issues.

3

Enjoying the Early Years

My early childhood years were fairly normal. I have many good memories of family and church and neighbors. I want to share some of those memories so you can see how God, with His faithful protection and healing, made a caring, nurturing situation possible for me in my early years. Additional medical challenges would arise in the future, but in these early years I didn't know anything about the challenges ahead. None of us did. We just enjoyed day-to-day life as I grew.

Mom would tell the story of my learning to walk at ten months, a bit earlier than most children. She said I would crawl backward from time to time and get my feet stuck under the couch. This would frustrate me so much that after doing it a few times, I just got up and walked. I was active and inquisitive. Mom took a photo of me at about a year and a half with the refrigerator door open, looking for something to eat.

Mom would dry clothes on a clothesline in the back yard. She would put the clothes in a bushel basket, put me on top, and carry me outside so she could keep an eye on me when she needed to do laundry. She took a picture of me in the basket, looking about as happy as can be. To avoid my abdominal scar line rubbing on the belt line of pants, I was always dressed in corduroy coveralls daily from ten months to three years old.

Mom also took another picture of me at about a year and a half standing in my blow-up wading pool. In this photo taken from the front, my scar line is clearly visible. What is also notable is the large indentation in my side. Doctors had removed the Wilms tumor in my second surgery, but in the process they had also permanently removed quite a bit of flesh. Since in effect my left side was caved in, the muscles in my side were not in the same orientation as God intended them to be. God also did not intend for us to have deep scar tissue, yet I had a significant amount in the affected area.

When I was around two my parents spent over one hundred dollars for orthopedic shoes, as did so many parents at that time. The first time they put these special shoes on me I decided to water the plants, and I doused the shoes along with them. Mom was too happy to have me around at all to be upset with me. She got the camera and took another picture.

On my second birthday, dad stopped on his way home from work and bought a red pedal fire truck for me. He intended to pay cash, but had stopped at the store on the spur of the moment. He asked the person operating the store if he would take a check. The response was, "Yes! People don't write bad checks for fire trucks." I eventually wore that fire truck out.

Close to the Land, Close to God

I would see my mother's father, my Grandpa Workman, from time to time. (My grandmother had passed away the year before I was born.) Grandpa lived about a hundred miles away. I remember one time when I was very little, not much more than two, climbing up on his lap. He had large ears. I reached up to his ear with my thumb and index finger spread apart to compare that span to his ear.

Grandpa Workman had a challenging life. Several members of his extended family wound up needing new places to farm because the farms they grew up on could not support them all. There was a section of land up for sale nearby that a lumbering company had cleared. Grandpa was part of a group of relatives who bought this land, divided it up, and put a dirt road down the middle. Grandpa's share of the land was 60 acres. The road is named after the family and is dirt to this day. It was almost like an early twentieth-century pioneer situation. My mom recalled the neighbors coming over for a barn raising when she was very little. Farming was done with horses for many years.

My grandparents' house had no running water, and cooking was done with an old wood stove like people had in the 1800s. There was no electricity until after Mom was grown. My grandparents raised eight kids during the Depression. In addition to my mother's medical issue, two of the other children also had medical issues that were taxing financially and emotionally. My grandparents' first child passed away in a crib death when she was three. Another child, one of my mom's brothers, passed away when he was eleven. Grandpa had a plaque on the wall over the table in the kitchen. It read, "As thy days, so shall thy strength be" (Deuteronomy 33:25 KJV). I still recall the look of delight he had on his face when I was on his lap, looking at his ear. Apparently, a grandchild responding to your love makes it all worthwhile.

I was blessed to get more than one taste of farm life in my early years. Our neighbors had a 40-acre farm. Mom would frequently push me in a stroller with large wheels down a path in their field. We would stop at the end of the path and sit on a large pink stone so I could watch their John Deere model B tractor in operation. When I was a little older we would both walk, but Mom would still bring a stroller along because I would almost always tire out and need a ride home. Mom wore out two strollers pushing me.

The First Florida Getaway

When I was two, Mom's doctor suggested she and Dad get away for a while. Dad worked in road construction and put in a lot of overtime. There was no time in the summer for vacations. But my parents took the doctor's advice and drove to Florida for a week in February. Very little of the interstate was complete, and part of the route was on steep two-lane roads that we would now consider backroads.

They spent the first night in Kentucky at a Ma and Pa motel. When they awoke, they found several inches of unexpected snow on the ground. As they ate breakfast, they watched several locals attempt to drive up the steep hill leaving town, and watched all of them slide back down again. Dad thought he could conquer the hill. He gave it a try and made it.

Later that day in the bottom of a valley in Tennessee, Dad and Mom found themselves in a long backup. The road they were traveling gained elevation as it went up a ridge of mountains and curved with the lay of the land. They could see the sides of motionless cars high on the ridge ahead of them, at least a half mile away. One of the locals came up on their left and said, "Follow me. I'll get you out of here!"

Dad followed this man's car into a farmyard. They drove right between the house and the barn, then down the dirt lane to the back of the farm. The lane met a dirt road that climbed the ridge on the opposite side of the valley from the main highway. A few miles later, this road tied into the main road at a point beyond the traffic backup. The whole trip turned out to be an adventure, and Mom came back rested.

While my parents were gone, I stayed with the neighbors who had the farm. As I grew up, this family treated me as one of their own. I would eat lunch at their house, and they would read me Bible stories from a book called *The ABC Bible Book*. They also gave me one of their much-used John Deere toy tractors and also a well-used Tonka truck their kids had outgrown. I used these toys in the sandbox Dad built for me in our backyard.

Over the years this family's kids, who were a few years older than me, practically adopted me. To celebrate my survival, they had a monthly "birthday party" for me until I was two years old. They would take me on horse rides. They had a dark blue 1948 Chevrolet truck their dad would let the oldest kids drive to the back of the farm, and I would get to ride along. Their grandmother had a simple cottage on a lake a few miles away, and my mom and I would often go with them to this cottage in the summer.

Faith's Firm Foundation

As a family, we would attend the little white church where I was baptized as a baby. In those days the church didn't have a nursery, so the toddlers sat through the main church service. When we were old enough, we went to Sunday school after the morning service. Old enough was very young, like a little before three years old.

I learned about God both at church and at home. One day the summer before I turned four, I saw my scar line scar in a new full-length mirror my mom had purchased. Confused, I asked my mom what it was. That was when Mom explained to me the basics of what had happened to me when I was born and that God had protected me through it. She told me many years later that Dr. Johns had advised her to wait until I asked before she explained what I went through as a baby.

I have vivid memories of Sunday school when I was three and four years old. We knew the leaders as Mrs. Uyl and Grandma Van Laan. Both of these ladies were probably in their sixties at this time, but to me they looked as ancient as the biblical characters they would tell us about. The stories were typical Sunday school stories such as Daniel and the Lion's Den, David and Goliath, the parting of the Red Sea, and Noah's Ark. These were taught, as well as stories of Jesus multiplying the fish and loaves, turning the water into wine, doing healing miracles, raising Lazarus from the dead, and walking on the water.

One Sunday, some missionaries came to Sunday school to explain their work. They showed slides of people in a foreign country, wearing white robes and being baptized in a river. This made quite an impression on me. The missionary testimonies and Bible stories were not just stories in my mind. These accounts of miracles and extraordinary faith were very real to me. That is really what Sunday school taught me—the basic truths of God's loving and caring for us and what our response should be.

On Pentecost Sunday when I was four years old, the pastor read the Pentecost story of the tongues of fire and the rushing wind. To me it seemed as if all the Sunday school stories and missionary presentations we heard were pointing to the Pentecost story. I thought, *Wouldn't it have been something to actually be there at the time and see the power of God!* By that point in my life, I knew enough about my medical past that I was able to understand that God had taken me through some really difficult physical circumstances. I knew God loved me. I knew the Pentecost story was real.

The Sunny Days

As I kept growing, life went well for several years. My aunt Maxine always seemed to take a special interest in me. She would always have a coloring book she could help me with or some small puzzles for me to put together. She would knit sweaters for me. When I would outgrow one, she would make me another. I still have the last one she knitted for me, just before she passed away. I was in high school at the time, so it fits me even now. On really cold winter nights, it is still ideal to wear.

On Sundays we would visit my dad's mother. Grandma Poll always had old-fashioned cookies and some pop for us. She had some old toys she had purchased when my cousins were little, a decade and a half before I was born. I particularly enjoyed two plastic toy trucks she had, because they were from the mid-1940s and were styled differently than the toy trucks that were popular when I was young.

Like most young boys, I felt my dad was my hero. When I was four or five, I would watch out the front window every night for him to get home. He worked in highway construction and the site would vary, so he might return home from any direction. Many nights, he would be turning in and I would see him at the last second because I was looking the other direction. I would get very excited! I would usually watch him back his truck into the garage, and I would rush out to meet him and carry his lunch pail as we walked to the street to get the mail.

One of my childhood books was titled *Good Night, Little Bear*. In the story the papa bear fell asleep in a chair, and the baby bear climbed up on his shoulders. When he woke up, papa bear pretended to not know where baby bear was and went through the house with him on his shoulders. Dad and I had our own version of the story. When it got close to bedtime, I would run to the bathroom and climb up on the counter. Dad would come into the bathroom and pretend not to see me. I would jump on his back, and he would run through the house with me on his back and tell me, "Remember to duck your head!" Then he would run under the bulkhead at the kitchen entrance. After some playtime together, he would read me a nighttime story. My favorites were *Buster Bulldozer* and *Corny Cornpicker Finds a Home*. I would have a snack, and then it was off to bed. Without fail, Mom would read me a Bible story and pray with me every night after she tucked me in.

When I was five, my parents announced that my mother was going to have a second child. I remember Dad carrying me to the neighbors in the middle of the night before he took Mom to the hospital. The next day, he told me I had a brother. After my parents brought my brother home, I stood looking at him lying in his bassinet. I had my ball hat on and I had a plastic ball in one hand and a bat in the other. I had seen the neighbor kids playing ball with a brother or sister, so I was ready to play ball with him. I remember thinking in that moment, *He won't be able to play ball with me!*

When I was six, dad was made a foreman for the road construction company. For several years, I would go with him on the road jobs from time to time on Saturdays. Most jobs were building interstate specification highways out of the bare earth. For me, it was a whole world of a bigger-than-life sandbox with the earthmovers and bulldozers in operation. I was able to see these close up as Dad drove through the job site in his four-wheel-drive foreman's truck and stopped to talk with different equipment operators from time to time.

The year my brother was born our family flew to Florida and stayed at the motel my parents had discovered there years before. I thought it was a wonderful place. It was built in the late 1940s a couple of blocks from the ocean in Fort Lauderdale, on highway A1A (now designated a Scenic and Historic Coastal Byway). The motel was actually two separate one-story buildings with four rooms each. They were flat roofed, cement stucco sided, and painted white with blue trim. All the windows were Jalousie crank windows—several strips of horizontal glass that would all crank open. The front door of the rooms faced a pool between the buildings. Bright sunshine would shine around the pool all day. Floating in the pool, you could see large palm trees that towered over the buildings. My parents would take us for long walks on the beach. I loved everything associated with the ocean, the salt air, the mystery of the tides, collecting shells, the palm trees, and the seagulls.

About the time I was seven, I needed new shoes. When I was young, I loved to run. Mom bought me a pair of PF Flyers. I remember looking at the treads on those shoes and thinking, *These will help me run so much faster!*

One day when I was eight, Mom had some business downtown. She decided to stop at the hospital and inquire if Dr. Wahby was available so she could show him how I was doing. He came out right away. He took a look at me and his eyes got big. He gathered everyone working in his department and had them come into the room. He kept pointing at me and saying, "I worked on him eight years ago, when he was a newborn!"

The lady who operated the cobalt 60 unit when I had been treated was still operating the same unit. She was especially thrilled to see me. She showed me the treatment room. I remember it being a fairly large room with dim lighting, and it felt a little cold. I also remember her pointing out the large, pea-green lead blocks on the walls and telling me the walls were four feet thick. She brought me into the control room and let me look through the small, thick window of leaded glass so I would have the same view of the treatment table as she once had when she was giving me the treatments. She asked if she could see my incision line. When I showed it to her, she was delighted that it had healed the way it did.

The first several years of my life were quite happy ones. I would be taken to Dr. Johns's office every six months for checkups and once a year for an annual physical. Dr. Johns was ideally suited to be a pediatrician. He was a man of Christian faith forged through the circumstances he had gone through. I do not recall him ever saying one word to suggest that any limitations I might have would ever hinder me from doing what I was intended to do in life. Yet my life was about to become more of a challenge. I knew my parents loved me, I knew God loved me, and I knew there was more to the Bible message than just simple stories. The firmness of that foundation would be challenged in the years ahead, yet in the end it would stand.

4

Another Unique Challenge

As I grew, the deep scar tissue in my side did not expand with my growth the way normal tissue would. One day just before my tenth birthday, I was late for the school bus in the morning and was running because the bus was waiting for me. The bus driver was a friend of my mom's, and she noticed that I did not have a normal stride when I was attempting to run as fast as I could. To her it looked as if I was really struggling.

The bus driver told Mom what she had seen. Mom set up an appointment with Dr. Johns, who looked me over closely. Dr. Johns ran his hand along my spine and noticed that my spine was developing a curvature. He referred me to Dr. Andre, an orthopedic doctor.

Mom had been the scrub nurse for several surgeries Dr. Andre had performed soon after she graduated from nursing school, so she knew him and felt she was able to trust him with my care. Dr. Andre ordered X-rays. He studied them carefully and determined that I had scoliosis, with a compound spinal curvature that was developing as I grew. The restriction of the scar tissue from those early surgeries was pulling my shoulders to the left and rotating my left shoulder forward and down. I had developed a sway to my back, and in addition, my left hip was higher than my right.

The challenge for Dr. Andre was to select a treatment for my worsening condition that would leave me with my back as straight and functional as possible when I was an adult. My parents were told it was not possible to do surgery to deal with the scar tissue. I was actually missing structure where the surgeon had removed the deep flesh where the Wilms tumor had been. This affected the area between the bottom of my rib cage and my pelvis on my left side. This flesh didn't grow back. Because of this condition, disturbing the area surgically would just result in more scar tissue, worsening the problem.

Limited Data, Limited Options

In those days, one option for dealing with scoliosis included surgically putting rods in the patient's back. This wasn't routinely done for a person at an age when rapid growth occurs, as I was. A second option was to have the patient wear a series of body casts as he or she grew, each cast staying on for up to six months. A third option was to fit the patient with a body brace of some kind. One brace was called a Milwaukee brace, which consisted of heavy material around the rib cage and steel stays with a framework extending up from it that would hold the head in a fixed position. Another brace was a simpler corset brace, which was fabricated out of heavy canvas containing vertical pockets into which steel stays were placed. A final option for treatment was to do nothing.

At first, Dr. Andre's plan was to use the body cast method on me. This would mean six months in a body cast, missing school, and going through rehabilitation to strengthen muscles not used for half a year—all followed by the possibility of another body cast being put on after the first one came off. Plans for this treatment were firm enough that my parents had fixed up my room. They installed carpeting and bought me a bunch of extra Lego blocks because it looked as though I would be in my room for at least six months. They anticipated that reading, creating things with Legos, and doing schoolwork would be the extent of my activities for quite some time.

Yet the proper course of treatment for my spine was debatable. Not much documentation was available on the history of treating patients in my condition. In fact, to this day, if another patient has ever existed who has a medical history with details fully paralleling mine, his or her story is unknown. Several things would have to line up. First would be simply having a Wilms tumor. Wilms occurs in 1 out of 10,000 births. The second would be early detection. In 1969, the National Wilms Tumor Study was launched to track medical data from Wilms patients. The data shows that with the technology available in the 1960s, being diagnosed at eight days old was almost statistically impossible. Early detection increased the likelihood of survival, but then scar tissue would form at an earlier age, which meant more distortion as a patient grew.

At the time of my diagnosis as a newborn, my tumor had been classified as a stage III tumor. The five-year survival rate for stage III Wilms patients, regardless of their age at detection, was under 10 percent in 1960, when I was born. Years later, I met a medical professional who told me her medical training had been in Europe in the early 1970s. She was taught then that a Wilms tumor was incurable. All of these factors contributed to my situation. But in 1970, there was no significant data on scoliosis induced by surgery and radiation in Wilms survivors available, so there was no textbook precedent set for its treatment.

When I look back on my course of treatment, it is clear that Dr. Johns had functioned just as much as a child psychologist as a pediatrician. He was constantly thinking about how a prescribed treatment would affect my daily life and outlook. Dr. Andre was considering the body cast option for me because it had been used on patients who were developing scoliosis without a direct traumatic cause, as in my case. But Dr. Johns' perspective was that I should be allowed to live as normal a life as possible while being treated. So he suggested the corset brace as an alternative, which was much like an old-fashioned ladies' corset. It was made of heavy fabric, with metal stays in long vertical pockets. This corset would extend from below my hip bone to an inch under my armpit. This offered several advantages over a body cast. The stays could be adjusted as I grew, I could take if off to shower, and I could continue most daily activities such as going to school while I wore it. Dr. Johns talked with Dr. Andre about all of this and he agreed, so they sent me to the brace shop to have a brace made. I was aware of the change of plan from body cast to using a brace. In my mind at the time, I viewed both plans as ominous and a bit abstract. The future looked like a big unknown either way.

The Brace Shop

The brace shop was in the basement of an ancient medical building next to Blodgett Hospital in East Grand Rapids. I remember that the staircase in the stairwell leading down to the shop had thick wooden handrails, with ornate metal posts holding them up. The brace shop itself was in a large, open room. It looked like a fabric store, except that all the materials in the room were off white in color. There were heavy duty sewing machines. There were headless mannequins of various sizes, so the people making a brace could match one of them up with measurements from a patient to ensure that a hand-made brace would fit. There were large rolls of heavy fabric, tables for measuring and cutting, machines to bend and form the stays, and also racks of various other materials used for patients with different needs, such as lifts for shoes.

On my first visit to the brace shop, I was shown a medical corset brace for the first time. Looking around as I walked in, I noticed a man working on an artificial limb. Seeing this stirred vivid emotion in me, and I wondered, *Am I going to become handicapped now?*

I realize the term *handicapped* has come to be viewed as offensive. When *handicap* was first used to describe a medical condition, the intent was to recognize a challenge a person had relative to his or her peers. This intent was similar to the way the word was used in sporting events such as golf and bowling, where a *handicap* accounts for differences in abilities and creates an equal chance of winning for each participant. However, saying that people with medical challenges had a *handicap* changed over time into using the term *handicapped* to describe the people themselves. Eventually, much of society began using the term *handicapped* to categorize people negatively when they did not measure up to set standards. Things started changing in the

1970s, as the word *disabled* started to replace *handicapped* in conversations. (Using the term *disabled* to describe physical challenges has also been criticized.) The passage of the Americans with Disabilities Act of 1990, with its resulting push toward focusing on people first instead of on their limitations, helped shift how society views people with physical challenges. But as a ten year old in 1970, my impression was that once a person was labeled as *handicapped*, he or she was in another world—at worst institutionalized, at best unable to participate in the meaningful things of society.

While I pondered the thought of how others would view me with a brace, a worker took several measurements of my back so that the hand-fabricated corset the shop was about to make would fit me properly. It needed to have the proper curves in the steel stays to prop my spine toward one side, which would influence the direction my bones were growing.

It took a couple of weeks for the brace shop to fabricate the corset for me. When your brace was completed, you didn't just go pick it up. It had to be fitted to you like a tailored suit, so I had to return to the shop for a fitting. You would wrap it around yourself and secure it using several buckles, much like a modern life preserver. The difference was that the buckles were the clinch type stainless steel, so for effectiveness it was important that everything was tight and fit correctly.

When we stopped at the shop to pick up my corset brace, the workers who had fabricated it put it on me. It was uncomfortable almost to the point of being painful the way it pushed on my spine. They took it off me and bent some of the stays. I thought they were trying to make it more comfortable, but they were actually bending the stays to give them even more leverage to push on my spine, which only increased the sensation! When we left the brace shop, it was late afternoon. On the drive home, I was trying to get used to the reality of wearing the uncomfortable brace I had on. My little league practice was that evening. Mom let me take the brace off for practice that day.

After that, it was down to business wearing the brace. I had it on at all times, even at night, except for taking a bath. That's when I started taking very long baths. The brace was a constant hindrance in my day-to-day activities. To achieve the purpose for which it was designed, it held my spine straight and did not allow my back to bend. At ball practice, attempting to field a ground ball was a challenge. Reaching down to the ground would cause the corset to dig into the front of my pelvis. If I happened to be lined up just right, with a ground ball coming at me, I could usually catch it. If the ball took a hop, I wasn't able to twist my body at the last second to get it.

Changes like that were going to take a lot of getting used to for me. They might seem like little things to most, but for me as a growing, active ten year old, the way the brace felt and the way it restricted my movement seemed huge. Beyond that, dealing with the implications of this whole situation and having to accommodate the brace in our day-to-day lives was going to be another challenge for our family!

5

Still in the Mainstream

I KNOW THAT AT THIS POINT MY PARENTS HAD TO MAKE A DECISION —to keep me involved in mainstream activities with the brace as a handicap, or to treat me like a handicapped person and pull me out of things. They chose to keep me involved in mainstream activities. They did a pretty good job with this. All they ever really asked of me was that I participate as best I could. They never pushed me to do more than my capability.

Many people who casually came in contact with me couldn't tell I was wearing a brace. One of the drawbacks of not drawing people's attention to a restriction you have is that you just don't know how they will react when they do find out. The photographer taking school pictures put his hand on my back when he went to turn me for a pose. I had no problem with that, but then he said, "Oh, you're wearing a brace!" He then apologized and acted as if he had hurt me.

On the other hand, one day Mom was at school working on a fundraising project. Looking out the window, she saw my class out on the playground for physical education class. The teacher had issues with some of the kids not putting forth much effort, so he had recently made it a policy to have all the kids run around the perimeter of the playground. Whoever came in last had to go around a second time. I was the one who had to go around twice. Every time. Mom had a few words with the teacher when she spotted that happening!

My routine visit with Dr. Johns was a couple of days after that incident. Mom told him what had happened. He responded, "It's a good thing you told his teacher not to do that. You don't punish someone for something they can't do."

In spite of the physical education issue, I actually have some good memories of that teacher. Even though he knew I was wearing the brace, he didn't stop to think that my condition might have been the reason I was the slowest. He didn't view me as disabled because of it.

In junior high, sports ability was an ever-increasing measurement of how students fit in with their peer group, whether it involved activities on the playground or organized sports. As the months moved on, it became obvious that I was in last place in all the sports activities we kids participated in. This caused me to start developing a resistance to the concept of being restricted. I turned the frustration into a resolve to be normal.

Another measure of fitting in with your peers was the way you dressed. Sleeveless muscle shirts were the popular choice of apparel in the summer. The brace had straps that came up over my shoulders, but the typical muscle shirt did not have shoulder straps wide enough the cover the straps on the brace. Mom spent quite a bit of time tracking down a type of shirt with extra-wide straps. Since the hook portion of the buckles on the corset would wear holes in my shirts quite quickly, Mom also learned to buy several shirts at once whenever she found a style that would work for me. Even with all of her efforts and all of mine, it was still a big challenge for me to feel as if I was measuring up.

From John Deere to Derby Car

Once in a while, there would be a bright spot. One of these was crop farming. Our neighbors with the farm moved out farther into the country, to a larger farm. They sold their house, but could not find a buyer for their land. They really wanted my parents to buy it, and the price was very low. Mom and Dad were in a position to do so. That seems odd with the large medical bill they had received just a few years prior, especially when their story was that they had only fifty dollars in the bank when they went on their honeymoon. Through dealing with challenging circumstances in earlier years, they had unknowingly prepared a way to pay the bill for my care. Or, perhaps more accurately, God was taking the circumstances and turning them for good. Dad used to tell the story about how they paid for their first house. He would say, "I was going to marry your mother, and I didn't have a dad around to guide me. I had some money [his army discharge pay], so I bought a lot, took a bulldozer home, and dug a basement. I bought the cement blocks and hired a bricklayer to put up the basement walls. I installed the sub-floor, and then I ran out of money. I thought I would get a loan from the bank. I went to two banks, and they told me they would not lend money on a new house not in a plat."

Then someone told Dad about a man in town who would lend people money. This man looked over the situation and asked Dad how much he needed to complete the next step. He then went to a safe in his wall, opened it, and counted out the money so Dad could continue building the house. The man kept careful track of what he had lent and all the payments Dad made.

My grandmother kept telling my dad there was going to be another depression and he had better get the house paid off. That became a focus for Mom and Dad. They paid it off a year and a half before I was born, even though it still lacked carpet, curtains, and a garage—all of which they would add and pay for before I was born. Their determination to have the house paid off worked out well when it came to paying my future medical bills, which they could not have anticipated. For a long time, I never found out what the total cost was for all of my medical care. Many decades after the fact, however, I did get Mom to tell me. After insurance, it amounted to a year's wages—about two-thirds of what their house cost.

Mom and Dad bought the neighbors' land. They also bought a small John Deere tractor, a model M, to put in a large garden. Whether we kids realized it or not, Dad was always doing things to teach and develop us. He would have me run the tractor, working up the land to prepare it for planting. The brace would dig into my pelvis when I got on and off the tractor and whenever I put the clutch in, but I loved operating the tractor! I wasn't going to let the brace stop me.

With the brace I couldn't bend over to pick crops, so Dad's idea was to turn me into a small-scale business manager. We contracted with a major canning company to grow pickles. We would plant three acres by hand. I built a stamper out of wood to poke holes in the soil so I could place and bury seed without bending over. A couple of neighborhood moms were looking for a little money and wanted to teach their kids to work, so we hired them to pick. Dad built a rack for the back of the tractor so I could haul the crop back to an old upright scale, where we weighed what each person picked. The canning company paid more per pound for the smaller pickles, so that was something I had to keep an eye on. At the end of the year, I had made enough from our farming activities to buy a new black three-speed Schwinn bike.

I used that new bike to prove to myself that I could do something athletic. Our house was at the base of a long, steep hill. I would ride to the top and wait for a time when no cars were coming. Then I would go as fast as I could down the hill. I would also ride the bike to my grandma's house and mow her lawn for her. She always offered me a dollar, and I always told her she didn't need to give me anything. Then she would insist I take the money. Quite a few evenings, I would ride my bike to her house and watch a ballgame on TV with her.

My mid-year checkup with Dr. Andre was scheduled on a beautiful summer day. It always seemed to me as though these doctor appointments took forever. Mom would drive us downtown, get parked, go up the elevator, and check me in. We would then wait to see the doctor. He would examine me and determine what X-rays he wanted taken this time. Then we would be sent to X-ray to wait. After a series of X-rays were taken, we would wait for them to be developed and for the radiologist to read them. We would wait again to meet with Dr. Andre, and he would then tell us what he had planned for the next treatment steps.

Between my body growing and the first brace's material wearing out, after a year it was time for a new brace. The new brace was of the same design but was larger, and for some reason it didn't seem as uncomfortable as the first one. After studying a fresh set of X-rays, Dr Andre also determined that I didn't need to wear the brace at night. That fact made wearing the brace much more tolerable on a day-to-day basis.

Even so, my frustration with being restricted by the brace continued to increase. One example of my continuing frustration was with little league. When I played right field and threw a ball to a baseman, I couldn't fully rotate my shoulders relative to my hips and I would tend to miss my target by a couple of feet. The brace also hindered my ability to take a good swing. I had no more than a couple of hits total in two seasons, and as I recall they were foul balls. When I was up to bat, the most I could hope for was to get a walk.

There was one game where we were behind by one point in the last inning, with players on base and two outs. I was up to bat. With two strikes against me, I swung and missed on the last pitch. As I was walking back to the bench, some of my teammates came up to me and said, "We lost the game because of you!"

I viewed this type of performance as a personal failure. The thoughts that came into my head were things like *You can't do anything!* and *You never will be able to do anything!* I watched the 1972 Olympics on our black-and-white television. Mark Spitz was the big story. When the swimming events were televised, one commentator was describing why a certain top competitor was so good. He said it was because this swimmer had long arms. *I have long arms*, I thought, *and I could go to the Olympics and win a medal, if it weren't for my side.*

Mom shared with me decades later that she and Dad often struggled with whether or not to keep me involved in mainstream activities. Their concern was that if I didn't participate, I might start viewing myself as not being capable at all. They felt if that attitude carried over into adulthood, then I wouldn't be able to provide for myself or have a family, etc. They thought a lot about how to help me through it all, and they continued to feel that keeping me in the mainstream was for the best.

Different situations would come up that validated their decision to keep me in the mainstream. One such situation came up at a birthday party for one of my classmates. Near his house there was pond the size of a hockey rink that was frozen over. His family had enough old ice skates for all the boys attending the party, and we played hockey. It turned out that he and I were the only kids who could do more than barely stand up on skates. I loved to ice-skate! It did not require significant twisting of my back and did not jar my spine. It gave me a sense of freedom. One time the creek by our house had been frozen, with no snow on it, and late one night under a full moon I skated that creek for miles. At the birthday party, literally skating circles around almost all the other kids as we played hockey was a good feeling!

Another bright spot for me came up when the boys' club at church held a Pinewood Derby race, something I could participate in without feeling physically restricted. I whittled my car with a jackknife. Dad thought earthmover axle grease would be just the ticket to make it go fast. Mom had a small kitchen scale that we used to weigh the car. To ensure that her scale was accurate, Mom called the local post office, which was housed in an old general store. They weighed pennies on a postal scale and we weighed the same number of pennies to verify her scale was accurate. The night of the race arrived. Round after round, my car kept winning. The final round came, and my car crossed the finish line almost half a car length ahead of the next fastest car. I came in first place!

Unrestricted Movement Moments

Another thing I could do, and enjoyed greatly, was ride the little red Honda CT 70 mini motorcycle my dad had picked up used. By then, my parents had sold their first house and had built a house on the farmland they had purchased. With trails connecting this farmland to other trails in the community, a person could ride for miles. Plus, the driveway to our new house was an eighth of a mile long and had a couple of twists and one large curve to it. I would spend hours seeing how fast I could get the Honda to go. I would start out by riding around the backyard to build up speed. As I reached the driveway I would be going about 10 miles an hour, and then I would open it up and see how fast I could go before I had to stop for the road. You had to take the large curve just right to make it, but I only wiped out once.

A couple of years after we got the Honda, I was adjusting the back brake and had the linkage apart. I went into the basement for a tool, and meanwhile Dad hopped on the Honda to get the mail. He was going about 35 miles an hour and was getting close to the road when he discovered he had no brakes. He made quite a swath in the neighboring wheat field after he swerved to avoid going into the road!

When I was eleven, Dad took a Friday off work to give us a long weekend, and our family went to the Straits of Mackinac to see the Mackinac Bridge and check out Mackinac Island. We decided to rent tandem bikes and ride around the island. While Dad was paying for the bike rental, I was staring through the bike shop window at what I thought was the most beautiful bike I had ever seen. It was a Schwinn Continental in a color called Sierra Brown, with a bit of metal flake in the paint. It was dim in the bike shop, but the Continental was right next to the window and was sparkling in the sunlight.

I looked at the Continental's price tag. To me, obtaining a bike like that looked about as possible as getting a new Corvette does now. Yet two years later, I had been working hard at saving money and had enough saved to buy a new Continental. I was outgrowing my three-speed, so I could justify getting a new bike. This was during the early 1970s bike boom. Demand for bikes was very high, and you couldn't just walk into a bike shop and walk out with a bike. I had to place an order with the factory for a Sierra Brown Continental in my size. Waiting five weeks for the bike to come felt like forever. Yet riding that bike once it arrived was worth the wait. It felt like being on a rocket, compared to my old three-speed.

Another memorable thing occurred during the time I was wearing the corset brace. It involved our annual family trip to Florida. Dad didn't like having to pay fifteen dollars a night for a motel room, and one year he had a brainstorm. Just after Christmas, he put an advertisement in the paper stating, "Wanted: Used Tent Camper." It was the middle of winter, so there was not much demand for campers in

Michigan. He got a few responses and found a two-year-old model at a rock-bottom price. He brought that camper home, cleaned it up and packed the wheel bearings. We took it to several locations in Florida. In central Florida we found a wonderful campground with two pools, a Dairy Queen, and orange trees on every campsite. Another location was a county park near the ocean, with big, open campsites. In the spring, Dad sold the camper and made enough money to pay for all of our trip expenses, plus he made a fifty-dollar profit! He bought and sold campers like this for several years.

We vacationed in Florida twice during the time I wore the brace. On those trips, I was able to take my brace off long enough to jump the waves in the ocean. The buoyancy of the salt water made this easy to do. It felt like being set free. (Perhaps that's why I still like to go jump the waves in Lake Michigan in the summer!)

27 Months and Then?

I ended up wearing a corset brace for a total of 27 months. My mother thought the brace had a significant effect on my spine. I am not so sure. I still ended up with a noticeable curvature of the nature I described earlier. At this point I had grown enough, however, that upon more careful examination Dr. Andre now found some strange things with my legs. He already knew that scar tissue had pulled up my left hip, causing my left foot to be closer to my nose than my right foot was. What he now discovered was that my left leg bones were actually longer than my right leg bones, but the difference in length did not make up for the amount my hip was up higher. A lift in my left shoe was considered, but while it might have improved my stride a bit, it would also have raised my left pelvis even higher when I was standing and walking. That would have enhanced the spinal curvature, creating more extreme muscular issues. There was therefore nothing more that could be done medically for me.

When it came to school and social situations, after the brace was gone I still faced some difficulties. The spinal curvature, the leg length imbalance, and the odd orientation of the muscles in my side had become a permanent situation that I did not want to accept. In just about every aspect my peers would judge me by, I would still come in last place. For instance, we had a rather small junior high school. I was one of the two people to get cut from the basketball team. The two of us were told we could go along to the games and be equipment managers. The other person who had been cut chose to do so. I did not. The idea of riding along on a bus with the rest of the class after hearing constant comments about my inability to play basketball did not appeal to me.

When I look back, I find it interesting that even though I was frustrated by the restrictions, never accepted them, and was not at peace with having them, I was actually letting them affect me. I viewed these restrictions as oppressing me. I came to the conclusion that God must love the other kids more than He loved me because He hadn't given them a curved back and a short leg. I truly did start to think of myself in terms of *I can't* and *never*.

My last year in junior high, the school started a soccer team for the first time. I got to be on the team. I played fullback, which didn't require much upper body coordination, the way basketball does. Mainly, it was just running straight at the person coming at me and getting the ball away from him. On the soccer field, I was motivated to prove to my classmates that I fit in. In fact, I did well enough to start part of the season. We even won the league trophy. In this instance, I appeared to became part of the mainstream successfully. Even while playing my position well, however, I would watch other kids scoring goals and know I wasn't capable of making the kind of moves it took to live up to that standard. So starting at fullback did little to affect my view of being restricted and not measuring up.

A few emotional bumps and bruises along the way are common for everyone, especially in junior high school. The truly damaging aspect of these events for me is how my view of God was shifting as a result. For the most part, the shift was so slow that I wasn't even noticing it at the time. Yet it would have an effect on me for years to come . . .

6

High School's Ups and Downs

High school gave me an opportunity for a fresh start socially. My high school was much larger than the junior high I had attended, so there were a lot more kids. I found a few new classmates with interests similar to mine, and I was becoming friends with a few people. Things were going well for me, and I was getting fairly good grades. I played my trombone as part of the marching band that performed at football games.

Then, in late winter of my freshman year, my urge to prove I could overcome any physical limitations flared up. Track season was approaching. The track coach held an informational meeting where he explained the practice schedule and gave everyone a handout detailing the track program. What caught my eye was a line item in the section on how track meets were scored. It contained a footnote stating three ways to earn a varsity letter. First, earn a certain number of points in a season by placing in events. Second, come within a certain percentage of the school record in an event. Third, participate every season and be awarded a varsity letter at the end of senior year.

I figured by getting a varsity letter I would prove that I was normal and didn't have any restrictions. All I would need to do was run fast enough in a single event. So I signed up for track and started showing up for practice. We would run four miles around a country block for a warm-up and do typical track workouts such as wind sprints and middle-distance repeats.

Developing my ability was an uphill battle. The coach was a good person. I obviously wasn't going to be his first choice for any particular event, however, so he placed me where he thought best for me. With the leg length issue, being a sprinter was not going to work out. With long distance, I would end up falling farther and farther behind in a race. So he put me in the 440-yard dash. There were multiple heats of this in a track meet, so I wouldn't end up competing directly with the fastest participants. Plus, the 440 was short enough that coming in at the back a few seconds after the rest of the field would not look so bad.

That season, I crossed the finish line in front of another competitor only one time. My best time for the year was many seconds away from the minimum time required for a varsity letter. At the end of the season the track coach encouraged everyone on the track team to participate in cross-country the next fall, to stay in shape for track. The cross-country coach gave us a handout with a suggested fitness program we could do over the summer to prepare.

My summer consisted of running to keep in shape, and also operating a tractor. The canning company quit contracting with growers in our area, so our agricultural focus shifted away from pickles. My dad bought a bigger tractor, a John Deere 60 with a three-bottom plow. I used this tractor to open up the soil and prepare most of the family acreage for winter wheat. After the initial plowing and a few passes with the disk, the ground was ready. Then all I had to do was pull a drag over the fields a couple of times a week to keep the weeds down prior to the fall planting.

I would run in the evenings. I had a friend from school who also was planning to join cross-country in the fall. We would both leave home at the same time, start running, and meet at a point about a mile from our houses. We would then run many miles out into the country. These long, leisurely runs went fairly well for me. They would jar my spine somewhat and cause some muscular issues to a degree, but the exercise felt tolerable for me.

6. HIGH SCHOOL'S UPS AND DOWNS

The Michigan High School Athletic Association did not permit team practice until a certain date, but we could prepare in other ways. The cross-country coach encouraged us to join the local track club, which held a few cross-country runs during the summer. Late that summer, word got around that we should all meet at school on a certain evening to go to a track club run. From school, we younger kids carpooled to the run with the juniors and seniors. This run was being held in a large county park where the lay of the land was interesting. Many big hills lay to the west. To the east lay flat bottomland that included baseball fields next to a big river.

This summertime event was held for running enthusiasts. This particular event was only for men. We signed in and had a few minutes to take in the situation. There were different age groups ranging from guys in their mid-teens through fifty-plus. My running partner and I had not participated in such an event before. There were at least a couple of hundred runners participating. We lined up near the back of the pack, behind the starting line at the edge of the ball fields. The gun sounded and we were off!

Going around the ball fields, the two of us were still near the back of the pack. As the pack spread out going up into the hills, we started falling to the very back. After a quarter mile, we were at the very back. Even the fifty-year-old runners were ahead of us. The course was very twisty and hilly, and before we made it half a mile not only were we last, but no one else was even in sight.

Since the pack was out of sight, we had to find our own way. Most of the course was on a mowed path about six feet wide that was normally used as a hiking trail. The route's marking was a bit haphazard, however, or perhaps we just didn't know what we were looking for. When different hiking paths crossed each other, it was not always immediately obvious whether to go straight or veer off on a crosspath. Often, the race markers were several feet beyond an intersection, which didn't help us any.

My friend and I continued to run on and on. At one point in a hilly section, the course straightened out. As we came over the top of one hill, we caught a glimpse of another runner's head disappearing over the hill ahead of us. I figured, *We're not as far behind as I thought!* When we arrived at the spot where we had seen the runner disappear, we discovered our trail dead-ended into a cross-trail with thick, heavy brush on the other side. We looked both directions and saw no markers and no runners. Glancing a second time to the right, we spotted the same runner topping another hill. We took off in that direction. A minute later, the course turned sharply and we were out of the hills and nearing the finish line.

A lot of spectators were there at the end, yelling and screaming. It was a relief when my friend and I made it across the finish line! Then I noticed something odd. The identical twins from our school, who had recently graduated after taking the school record back and forth from each other in their last cross-country season, were there to run for fun and had finished ahead of us. They were standing beyond the finish line with just a handful of other runners, watching for the main pack to come in. I looked behind me, and here came the pack! Two of the people leading the oncoming wave were from our school. They were destined to be the top runners from our school in cross-country that next fall. One ended up being all-conference. The other was all-state and eventually went on to the Olympics, where he won a bronze medal.

I recall my friend and I coming in eighteenth and nineteenth at that event overall. We later found out that after the course we were supposed to run on left the ball field, it went up into the hills and returned for another lap of the ball fields before going back into the hills and following multiple trails. By misreading the course markers, we essentially took a dramatic shortcut and unintentionally cut back into the pack between the race leaders and the main pack—all without being noticed! The coach was there as a spectator, and he thought he had a couple of future superstars on his hands when we crossed that finish line. We were too embarrassed to tell him what had really happened.

That run turned out to be quite taxing on my body. On the uneven terrain each stride would jar my spine. When my left foot hit the ground, my spine would jar one way. When my right foot hit it the ground, my spine would jar another way. I decided that pursuing cross-country simply wasn't worth it for me. My friend, however, went on to develop himself into a respectable cross-country runner.

I also rethought participating in track the next year. It was obvious that the only way for me to get a varsity letter was to stick with the program until I graduated. It would be awarded as a participation award for showing up every season, not because I was actually able to live up to the standard. I decided not to show up for track practice again.

Truth Misapplied

As I was dealing with whether or not to give up on "proving" I was normal and could measure up to what a normal person could do, I started to do some real thinking about why I had ended up short-changed, as I saw it, compared to the people around me. I started filtering what I read in the Bible through my experiences, and I started developing my personal theology further to explain what I saw. I would look at statements in the Bible that are clear and absolutely true and misapply them to my life.

My thoughts went like this: *God is almighty, and not a hair can fall from our heads without His will. He knit me in my mother's womb. He predestines things. So He must have wanted me to have the Wilms, the brace, the scar tissue, the curvature, the short leg, and the limitations.* At the same time, I knew God had brought me through medical challenges that were almost statistically impossible to overcome. I also had been taught that God has a covenant with His people to be a God to them and their children.

The best way to describe my resulting perspective was that I viewed the Kingdom of God like the public school system. God was the bus driver. Life was like getting up in the morning, getting on the bus, and traveling to school. School was like heaven, and you don't want to miss heaven. Since I was part of the covenant I was in the district, so God had to pick me up and provide the basics for me, even if He didn't like me that much. On the way, the bus driver might hit a few potholes and hit the brakes hard from time to time. That would affect everyone who had day-to-day challenges. It seemed to me as if I had purposely been placed in the back of the bus, where the bumps feel bigger and you get more thrown around going around corners. Someone has to be in the back of the bus, and the driver doesn't really care who it is or how rough the ride, as long as you get to school.

With that mindset, I would actually end up hearing something different from people than what they actually spoke. Dr. Johns once said to me, "God must have a real purpose for you to have brought you through all this." I would have told you that he said, "God must have had a real purpose to give you all this." By just shifting, omitting, or adding a few words in my mind, my understanding of what people said could be very different than what they actually said.

My mindset also prompted me to give up on trying to fit in by proving something. Soon, an opportunity came up that would give me an excuse not to be involved in school social activities anyway, so I took it. As I was nearing my sixteenth birthday, I developed a strong desire to get a car. Dad told me that *car* was spelled *J-O-B*. Since I wasn't going to be involved in sports anymore, I had no demands related to practice after school. That meant I could look for a job.

Becoming a Bagger

Before long, I applied for a job bagging groceries at the local grocery store. I was offered the job at a pay rate of $2.38 an hour. Typical hours would be 5:00 p.m. to closing at 10:00 p.m. twice a week, plus random hours on Saturdays. This was enough to enable me to buy a car, pay the insurance, buy gas, and save a little bit of money.

There were close to twenty part-time bagger employees like me at the store. A few other kids from my school had the same position. They would treasure a Friday night off in the winter so they could go to a basketball game, especially homecoming. If I wasn't scheduled on a Friday, I would swap to let another bagger have the night off. I went to only one basketball game the whole time I was in high school.

I worked part-time at the store during both the school year and

6. HIGH SCHOOL'S UPS AND DOWNS

the summer. When not at the store during the growing season, I would be working with the farm equipment. One of the highlights for me was bringing the wheat harvest to the grain co-op midsummer. I made several thirty-mile round trips with the John Deere 60 to deliver the harvest. The tractor was tricky to operate with a full load. It had a hand clutch, and you selected one gear. No upshifting after you were rolling. I would ease the tractor and wagon onto the shoulder of the road in front of our fields. It sloped slightly downhill. I would put one foot on each of the wheel brake pedals, put the gear selector in sixth gear, and run the hand throttle up to full position. I would take my feet off the brake pedals and ease in the hand clutch. The engine would lug down, and the front end would jump up and down a bit. I would snap the clutch in place, and I was off at 17 miles an hour! Watching the grain slide down the chute at the grain elevator and taking home the weigh ticket really made me feel that I was part of American agriculture.

Working at the grocery store was a developmental experience. I would help people find items they needed and load groceries in their carts as they checked out. I would also have short interactions with them as I bagged their groceries. The store was part of a small chain. One time, the president of the organization held a meeting with the baggers in the conference room of a hotel. He told us, "You are the first and last people our customers see. How you treat them is how they see the company." This helped shape how I have approached people on behalf of my employers or the volunteer organizations I have been involved with throughout the years.

I didn't just bag groceries, however. I would also round up shopping carts, stock sales specials and the dairy case, wash trays in the bakery, and sort pop bottle returns. We baggers had some fun doing that. The bottle sorting area was cramped, so at times we left racks of sorted bottles outside until closing. From time to time, we would think we heard people stealing the bottles. If I heard any suspicious sounds out there, I would round up a couple of other baggers for support and we'd quickly swing open the door, hoping to catch a bottle thief in the act.

We never did, until one day when I heard suspicious sounds out by the racks similar to what we had heard before. Wanting to have some fun, I called to another bagger, "I think we've got someone stealing bottles!" We really didn't expect to find anything wrong, but we quickly swung open the door and yelled, "Got ya!" We found three guys, each about twice our size, standing by a car with the trunk open. They were holding cases of pop bottles they were about to steal. In the moment, seeing their size, I thought, *This was not a smart thing we just did!* Fortunately for us, these big guys were more afraid of the situation than we were of them, and they took off.

The store employees had their own social structure. On Saturday night after the store closed, we would go out for pizza as a group. Every week, the pizza place would set up for us with a long table. We all knew about what the total bill would be, and we all pitched in to cover it. We would debate about what to order, but we always ended up ordering the same thing. It seemed as though everyone was on a level playing field, and everyone had a good time.

Senior Year's Snowstorm

In the winter of 1978 I was in my senior year of high school. That winter is forever etched in the minds of people who lived through it in West Michigan. We had a massive blizzard. One January evening when the weather was quite mild, the barometer began to drop very quickly. I read once that it was fastest drop ever recorded outside the tropics.

Heavy snowfall and sustained high-speed winds resulted, with occasional gusts of up to 120 miles an hour. The snow was flying horizontally. Our house in the country ended up with an eight-foot-high drift around it. On the interstate, one interchange was located at some open farmland and was completely blown shut with snow as deep as the overpass bridge. From the air, it wouldn't have appeared that there was even a highway there. Everyone was snowed in for at least two days. The manager of the grocery store called me and said, "If you can get here, we can use you."

We managed to clear our driveway, and Dad drove me to work in his red Chevy four-wheel drive foreman's truck the second day after the storm. It was calm by then. However, deep snow still clogged the streets and highways, and abandoned cars that had become stuck in the snow early in the storm hindered the cleanup effort. The store had not had any delivery trucks come in. Yet bundled-up customers pulling their sleds and toboggans were arriving at the store. As far as normal staples go, only a few loaves of bread and a couple of gallons of milk were left on the shelves. The few of us employees who had come in worked on getting things back to normal. We mopped the floors and finished cleaning snow off the entry areas. We also bagged items for customers who made it into the store. With most of the staples sold out, they were buying items they rarely bought to stock up, so they would have food for a few days until the roads were cleared.

After the roads were cleared, you had to dig down to open up your mailbox. Drivers could not see crossroads over the snowbanks. An unofficial code of driving ethics developed. If you lived in the suburbs, you would always have a minimum of two people in a car. At a stop sign, the passenger would get out and look over the top of the snowbanks for cars. You waited to make trips after dark if you were driving alone. Then you could see car lights shining into the sky behind the dark snowbanks, so you knew a car was coming.

This blizzard came long before cell phones. In those days, you just didn't leave home without a shovel, a blanket, extra clothes, and a bag with food and drink in it. (Still a good idea.) Gatorade was popular because it didn't freeze as fast as water. For the next several weeks there was no guarantee you would make it home from any outing, due to the conditions left in the storm's wake.

Senior Year's Success

To meet a class requirement during my last year in high school, I wrote a paper entitled "The Power of the Mind to Heal." Most of the sources I found in my research dealt with the mind-over-matter principle. I did find one source that documented something unusual.

An experiment was conducted where DNA was irradiated, scientifically examined, and documented to be damaged. After that, a person placed his hands on the container of the irradiated material and prayed. Then the DNA was again examined and was found to be repaired. I found that report fascinating. I didn't recognize it at the time, but now I believe what sparked my interest in the article was also what motivated me to respond to the Pentecost sermon the way I had when I was four years old.

As my high school career drew to a close, I received a State of Michigan Competitive Scholarship based on my ACT score. Although I did fairly well in school, I never made the Honor Roll. What is strange is that I scored very high on the ACT. I received a letter from *Who's Who Among American High School Students* saying they were going to list me due to my score.

I have often wondered why my grades were lower than my ACT scores suggested that they should have been. Perhaps the fatigue my mother noticed when I was little had affected my schoolwork all along? Yet one way or another, I had made it through high school and had come out the other side with a diploma in my hand. As I continued working my job at the grocery store that following summer, I knew the time had come to take another step . . .

7

Building Roads and Romance

The summer after graduating from high school I signed up for a trigonometry class at the junior college to complete a prerequisite for calculus. It was an enjoyable experience. One section of the building was very old. The entrance was through large, heavy wooden doors with several marble steps going up to another set of the same doors. I reflected on how many people had walked up those steps in the many decades that the building had been there. I knew Mom had taken classes there as part of her nurses training and had walked through the same doors.

In the fall, I enrolled in Calvin College. The college had a student body of four thousand. It was only a twenty-minute drive to school, so I avoided the cost of dorm fees by commuting. I aspired to be a doctor, despite my average grades in high school. I would like to believe this was inspired by Dr. Johns. He did a lot of good for a lot of people, and I wanted to do the same. Or perhaps it was inspired by wanting to overcome what appeared impossible and prove something?

Calvin College had a requirement that all students must successfully complete two years of a foreign language to graduate. I had taken one year of Latin in high school. Being advised that it would be best to study a language that was currently in daily use, I chose to take German my first semester. I also signed up for calculus, chemistry, and ancient history. The time commitment required to complete the coursework in these subjects pretty much would fill a person's schedule entirely. However, I also still had my job at the grocery store. Most days, it was quite late before I really had time to sit down and study. Usually, I was too fatigued to concentrate properly.

Looking back, I suspect that the tension in my muscles, which was caused by the scar tissue from my early surgeries, contributed to an abnormal level of fatigue. Simply being in a seated position would subject my spine to being pulled to the left by the scar tissue tension, to a greater degree than when I was standing and moving. I didn't recognize this at the time. I had been dealing with the scar tissue tension my whole life. How was I to know just how much of a challenge I had, compared to what other people faced? Needless to say, with feeling like that while taking those types of classes throughout the school year and working on the side, I wasn't at the top of my college class when it came to grades.

Joining the Road Crew

Just as the school year was finishing up, I applied to work at the road construction company where my dad worked. If hired, I could make more in the summer than I made all year at the grocery store. This would free me up to study during the school year. I was hired in and gave my notice at the store. Joining the road crew, I was assigned as general labor on a project building US 131. The construction site was an hour's drive from home. This road was built to interstate standards, and it was a "green field" project—building from scratch out of the bare earth. It would take three years total, and I was joining the crew at the start of the second construction year. The previous year, the land had been cleared. The topsoil had been removed and stockpiled, hills along the route had been cut out, and two of the four bridges had been completed.

A typical summer day that year started at 5:00 a.m. with driving to a carpool lot. Several of the workers would meet there and drive to the town near the job site. We would arrive just before 6:30 a.m. and have the $1.50 breakfast at the Legion hall. We were on the job site at

7. BUILDING ROADS AND ROMANCE

7:00 a.m. Coffee break was ten minutes at 10:00 a.m., and lunch was an unpaid half hour at noon. Quitting time was 5:30 p.m. The drive back was through the end of rush-hour traffic as we neared Grand Rapids. I would arrive home just before 7:00 p.m.

On the project site, I did a variety of jobs. One was using a chainsaw to clear the path for the fencing that goes along the right-of-way. Another was dealing with topsoil. When topsoil was placed on banks, I would finish leveling it by hand with a large rake. We had one bulldozer operator who was so good at running a little John Deere 350 wide-track bulldozer that he would know exactly how much topsoil was in front of this blade. There were times when he would flick the blade and the dirt would fall perfectly in place around the bell of a drainage pipe. When this happened, all I had to do was smile at him.

Another job I did was checking the grade. As part of the project, a new access road was built alongside the new highway. The sand fill had been placed, and the equipment operator and I were using a big Caterpillar 16 grader with wide sand tires to grade the sand. Grading with precision was important. It put the level of sand exactly where the engineers intended it to be for the finished road after the gravel and blacktop were added, so the surface would be smooth and rainwater would run off properly.

The survey crew put stakes on each side of the road every 50 feet, with grade markings. My job was to check that the finished level of sand was correct. I would take two metal rods connected by a string and push them in the ground next to stakes placed on each side of the road. The rods had markings on them that I would line up with marks on the stakes. The string was 12 inches higher than these marks. I would measure the distance from the string to the surface of the sand near both edges of the road and in the center. We had a system where I would mark in the sand with my foot, indicating how many inches needed to be cut to get the proper grade. I would remove the rod and string. The grader operator would make a pass. I would reset the string and verify that the grade was correct, and we would move on.

There were large ridges of sand on both sides of the road, so it turned into a workout for me climbing over these all day. This did wear me out by the end of the workday, but the effort didn't require much twisting of my upper body, so I didn't perceive any significant fatigue due to musculoskeletal tension. Most of my physical activity that summer actually improved my condition because it resulted in strengthening the muscles that supported my spine.

One day, we were using a hydraulic excavator to excavate an area that two 60-inch-high pressure gas lines passed through. The gas company required notification if we worked in such an area and sent two inspectors to watch us work. My role was to watch how close to the gas lines we were coming after each scoop of the excavator bucket. I thought it was a little odd when the inspectors sat on a distant hill and watched us through binoculars as we worked near the pipe. How were they supposed to see what we were doing from so far away? A few days later, I was watching the national nightly news when I got home from work. There was a film documenting a construction crew in Texas who had hit the same type of gas line with an excavator. The machine had been abandoned and was engulfed in a huge ball of flame. Apparently, the inspectors on our site were there to radio in a request to shut off the gas flow if we hit a pipe!

The crew with the earthmovers and bulldozers spent the early part of the summer putting 75 feet of sand fill in place to create bridge pads for the foundations for bridge abutments. The bridge crew poured the concrete footings and walls. My foreman dropped me off at the site with a 10-gallon gas can and a walk-behind vibratory packer. The big, lime-green Terex TS-24 earthmovers would pull nose first up to the inside of the wall and ram-dump their loads, back out, and go for another load. A bulldozer operator would spread out the sand and run back and forth on it to compact it. There were two side walls, as well as the end wall. The bulldozer operator could not run right along the walls, however. My job was to operate the vibratory packer and get compaction along the walls. The packer was a heavy machine about the size and shape of a walk-behind lawn mower.

The sand fill was put in place in 1-foot lifts. An inspector would use a nuclear testing device to test the density. The testing device contained a radiation source in the bottom of a retractable tube. The inspector set the instrument on the surface of the sand, released a catch, and pushed the tube into a hole he had made in the sand. The bottom of the device contained a sensor that measured radioactivity traveling from the tube through the sand. The electronics in the device would calculate what the density of the sand was, based on how much radiation it had blocked.

When we started, the distance to the top of the wall was over 25 feet. The sand would be placed. I would run the compactor on the edges while the bulldozer operator compacted the sand. A foot at a time, we went up the inside of the walls, with the inspector completing a test for each foot we compacted. Late in the day, we had filled enough so that I could look over the top of the wall at the surrounding woods. One time an earthmover operator pulled up within a foot of my arm when I was looking away. He opened up the V12 Detroit Diesel engine to ram-dump his load. I almost jumped over the wall when I heard this and saw the huge machine so close to me. Then I saw that the operator had a big grin on his face!

Dad was in charge of several road jobs around the state and would visit our construction site once or twice a week. He was careful not to get too directly involved with me, and he left my supervision to one of the foremen working for him. One Friday night, he came by around quitting time. "Why don't you ride home with me?" he asked, so I did. As I got into his Chevy El Camino, he said, "I've got a few things I need to check out."

The bridge crew was planning on delivering the huge steel beams for our new bridge. Dad wanted to inspect the smaller county bridge on the route to the job site to make sure it would not collapse under the weight of those beams. We climbed into the ditch at the side of the road and got right under that county bridge. Dad commented, "I think we'll be all right. The last thing you want to do is have to buy the county a new bridge!"

There were a couple of other things Dad needed to attend to, expanding my ten-hour workday that day to twelve. Those last two hours did not go on my timesheet. Those were the hours Dad kept. He worked those kinds of hours until he was sixty-seven. The last year he worked, he would wake up before his alarm during the construction season and be gone by 5:00 a.m., returning home no earlier than 7:00 p.m.

During that time frame, I had been thinking about buying a newer car. Dad had spotted a deal on a lot in one of the towns we went through on the way home. We wandered around the dealership lot. They were offering a deal on a brand-new Camaro. With what I made that summer, I could have bought it with cash, but I decided that having a bit of financial security was more important than a new Camaro. I kept my 1971 Impala.

That fall at my annual physical, Dr. Johns asked me what I had been doing. I told him about working on the road crew. I mentioned that the construction work did not jar my spine and cause musculoskeletal issues nearly as much as running or working with things over my head. His response was, "When you are in college, letting your mind rest and being on the end of a shovel in the summer is one of the best things you can do." I figured he should know. He told me he had worked his way through college by working in a coal mine.

Back at Calvin College that second fall, I was charging on with premed classes. I was enrolled in German, cell biology, organic chemistry, and economics, as well as physical education. All students were required to take physical education for one semester. The goal was to expose us to different activities and encourage us to find enjoyable ways to keep physically fit throughout life. I made a good move and signed up for this class in the fall. After working on the road crew all summer, I did well on the baseline test the first week.

Kindred Spirits

My cell biology class had a lab session that met one afternoon each week. The room was arranged with tables seating four students each. I came into the room and spotted someone who had gone to my high school, so I sat next to him. Across from us were two girls. One I knew from my church. The other I had not yet met, as was common beginning a new year at college. She introduced herself, and her name was Beth. She grew up fifty miles from the school, was staying in the dorms, and was planning on entering the BSN (Bachelor of Science in Nursing) program.

At the end of the first lab session, the professor encouraged the students at each table to get to know each other by sharing their academic goals with each other. I shared that I wanted to be a doctor and then did something I rarely did. I shared my medical history to explain my motivation for meeting my goal. I even pointed out the indentation in my side and the shift in my spine.

Beth and I started chatting a lot during our lab sessions. After a few weeks, I asked her out on a date. As we got to know each other, we were quickly more drawn to each other than attracted to each other. We were like the salt and pepper figurines that my grandmother had. When I was little, I would play with these figurines, which were held together by magnets. I would slowly move them closer to each other, until suddenly they would come out of my grasp and snap together on their own.

Beth and I had a lot in common. She never quite fit in with her peers growing up and also faced a few academic challenges in high school. When she was younger, she had an uncle who was frequently hospitalized for asthma. Visiting him in a large Grand Rapids hospital inspired her to become a nurse and work in a similar setting. She was on her high school track team and set the school record in the 100-yard dash. She was anchor leg on the 440-yard relay at the regional state qualifying meet. She was slightly behind a competitor coming to the finish line when she strained for the tape and fell. The hospital had to dig pieces of the track out of her skin. I could tell she had that kind of resolve to overcome obstacles.

Beth was very attractive, but I never really thought about her looks. I just thought it was normal for girls to look like the models in clothing catalogs. After our third date I had not proposed, but it was obvious to both of us that we would be sticking together. We found inexpensive things we really liked to do for dates. One of the most memorable was going to the beach at Lake Michigan when there was a foot of snow on the ground and having a picnic. Roasting hot dogs on a cold beach warms you up!

Academic Challenges

That semester when we met was a struggle for both of us academically. I began to realize that medical school was unlikely for me. Beth did not do well in two of her classes, so it was a period of uncertainty for her as well. She knew she needed better grades, and she did not want to fall short of becoming a nurse. It began to look as though becoming accepted into nursing school wasn't going to happen and she would have little option but to return home and become a nurse's aide at the tiny local hospital where she had been a candy striper in high school.

By the end of the school year, I made the decision to complete a science degree and see where that would lead me. Beth had her own situation to deal with. Students applied to the BSN program after two years of college. There were limited openings, and acceptance was based on very competitive academic standards. Should she take some classes over and apply at the two-year mark? She consulted a student advisor and was told that the BSN route was unlikely to work out for her. She was advised to enroll in a hospital-based RN (registered nurse) program the next year.

Beth applied to the Blodgett Memorial Medical Center School of Nursing program. If accepted, she would take some academic classes at Calvin College and nursing classes at the hospital. She met all the prerequisite requirements of the program except one. She needed a minimum grade in a certain type of chemistry class. Beth enrolled in the local junior college near where I grew up for a summer chemistry course. She was going to stay with her brother, who was renting a house with some roommates in an area of town that was considered unsafe. The second night Beth stayed there, she called our house and said she thought she had heard gunshots. My parents asked her if she wanted to stay at our house instead for the next few weeks. Beth had spent quite a lot of time at our house the previous semester, especially on weekends, so everyone was comfortable with this arrangement.

Early that summer, I took two physics classes to get them out of the way. The professor had an unusual background. He had been in the Air Force, preparing to be a pilot, when the Vietnam war came to an end. The Air Force redirected him to the Air Force Institute of Technology, where he earned a master's degree in physics. He came to know Jesus as his Savior at the institute. While teaching physics, he was attending the local Baptist seminary to prepare to go on the foreign mission field. The first day of class, he looked at us through his fighter pilot glasses and said, "This summer we are going to learn physics and go through the book of John."

The way this professor emphasized that studying the book of John had the same seriousness as the course material in physics really impressed me. These were accelerated classes. We had class all morning and lab most of the afternoon. Evenings were dedicated to homework. I did well in those classes.

Back on the Road Crew

After that, I was back to the road crew. The job I enjoyed the most that summer was laying pipe. The trench would be excavated, and we would set up a laser aligner to verify that the trench was the correct depth. When we were laying concrete pipe, we would throw a cable over the pipe and hook the cable to an excavator bucket. The excavator operator would place the pipe. A laser target would be placed in the pipe to determine if the pipe was aligned. Usually, we would use big pry bars to manually align the pipe section. A loader operator would shake sand into the trench alongside the pipe. We would then spring into action and shovel sand under the outside curvature of the pipe.

To get compaction we would operate a device known as a "pogo stick," only it wasn't a toy! This was an air-operated device that weighed about 35 pounds. It was 3 ½ feet high, with a heavy plate on the bottom. At the top there was a lever to activate it. When activated, the plate would be forced down by the air and then would retract. As long as the lever was engaged, the plate would keep jumping. I would carry the pogo stick into the trench with the 2-inch airline over my shoulder, hold it at a 45-degree angle under the curvature of the pipe, and hold the trigger. One hot August day, the type where I would drink a gallon and a half of water by the end of it, I operated the pogo stick on both sides of a 100-foot trench. When I was finished, my legs felt like spaghetti. One night after a day like that, I got home from the road job and was all dirty. Beth had been in her hometown for a while after completing her chemistry class and had not seen me like that before. She pulled into our yard just as I was getting out of my car, and she just stared at me. My dad said, "Go ahead and give him a kiss!"

One afternoon when we were laying pipe, I was down in the trench and the operator of the Insley H-1000 excavator moved the machine a few feet farther down the trench. I did not see that it had moved. When he swung the crane around, the counterweight of the machine hit my hard hat and knocked it off my head. This was the closest I came to a serious injury in the road-building business.

The first thing you are taught on a road crew is: "Don't get separated from your lunch pail." The lunchtime venue would vary depending on where you were working on the job when lunchtime came. One day, two of us on the crew climbed up to the short, flat spot under one of the new bridges to eat lunch, where it was cool. My favorite spot, however, was under an apple tree next to a creek. We had installed a pipe under the road to carry the creek. The bank around this had been sodded to prevent erosion. Next to it was an edge drain we had installed to remove groundwater from the soil under the roadbed. There must have been springs in that soil. The drain was constantly flowing with the best-tasting cold water you could imagine. Everyone working on the job would stop and refill their water jug from this edge drain.

That year, I drove myself to the job, and I had fun going home at night. The state staggered completion times of projects due to budgeting concerns. Another company had completed the four miles of road to the south of our job a year before we completed ours. The two projects were scheduled to be open to the public at the same time. That summer I had four miles of brand-new, unopened highway all to myself on the way home. It had not been striped, and there were no speed limit signs! I was careful, of course, to get back down to the speed limit when the road tied in with the existing highway.

7. BUILDING ROADS AND ROMANCE

With working so many hours, Beth and I did not get to see each other much during the week. On Sunday afternoons we would walk back in the field to a big maple tree and climb up onto a platform the neighbor kids and I had built many years before. This was a peaceful place of refuge. The tree stood alone on the edge of the field. The neighbor's land next to it was pasture on a piece of high land, with lowland and a creek winding through it. Two hundred yards away was a large section of woods. On the platform in the tree, we were surrounded with huge limbs reaching to the sky and reaching out below us. The leaves were thick, but there were small patches of blue sky visible through them. The wind would gently blow the leaves, and we would lie on the platform and watch the motion of the leaves and the patches of clouds moving through them.

In the fall it was time for another year of school. I continued on with my science classes. The college was a liberal arts college, so along the way I took a variety of classes. The strange thing is, I enjoyed economics, history, and psychology more than the science classes. In fact, in every psychology class I took I earned a 4.0! I also took a history of England class. For my term paper I tied my interest in road building to English history by researching Roman roads in England. One history journal had diagrams of how the storm sewers there were designed and built out of stone, with no mortar. Years later, I was able to see the same construction in some Roman ruins in Spain.

Beth had gotten an A on her required chemistry class and was accepted into the hospital RN nursing program. Her nursing classes were held on the top floor of the same ancient medical building that housed the brace shop that made my corset braces. With the hands-on approach of this type of nursing school, things went well for her.

Beth and I would spend a lot of evenings studying together in the college library. We had a table we liked all staked out. Since we were always looking for a good cheap date, we would take advantage of steak night Friday evenings at the college food service. Beth had a meal plan, so she was covered. I just had to come up with two dollars for my meal.

Life at Full Throttle

The winter break of my junior year, we spent quite a bit of time snowmobiling. We would pull each other on a "track" in our alfalfa field. We would also take a trail to Dutton Park. This park had a hill-like mound fifteen feet high. We would go up over this just fast enough with the snowmobile to jump a tiny bit and slap the track as we went on the downslope. One night we were snowmobiling on a big field near the park. As we were going along, another snowmobile pulled even with us and then started to pull ahead. This meant, *You can't beat me!*

I pulled the throttle all the way back, Beth hung on, and we pulled ahead of the competition. He was not too far behind as we neared the park. I yelled to Beth, "Do you want to go for it?"

Beth enthusiastically yelled back, "Yeah!"

We went into the park at full throttle and hit the hill. I still remember the feeling of floating and watching our headlight beam tracing a path from top to bottom on the chimney of a house on the other side of the park. We never touched the other side of the hill. We landed on flat ground beyond it. I slowed quickly to miss a creek. Then I swung the snowmobile around and pointed it in the direction we had come. A few seconds later, the other snowmobile came over the top of the hill very slowly. He probably was looking for our wreckage.

At the close of the school year Beth got a nurse's aide job at a nursing home. I took a short course at the junior college to complete a general education requirement. It was a music history/appreciation class. I would read the book and study as usual. The professor would grade on a curve. He would take the highest grade on a test and set that equal to 100 percent. I would score between 96 and 100 percent on a test. The next-highest score would typically be in the high eightieth percentile. My classmates were not very happy with me. I asked them if they had read the book. It was nice to be at the top of the class for once.

After my class was finished, it was off to the road crew. The project

I had worked on the previous two years had been completed. This summer, we were working on the same road just fifteen more miles from home. My total time away from home each day was actually a little shorter because we put in eight-hour days instead of ten.

This was another job requiring laying lots of pipe. One pipe was made of large, corrugated steel eight feet high. It would carry a small creek bed under a service road. The challenge was that the road had to be a certain height above the creek, and the pipe had to be wider than the creek to handle seasonal water runoff. The engineers specified a wide pipe. One-third of it was to be below the stream bed. The pipe was installed, and three of us would shovel gravel into wheelbarrows, push them into the pipe, dump them, come out, and start over. This was not leisurely gardening—it was production! One of the people I worked with said, "When I got called back to work this spring, another pipe like this was the first project I was on. That night when I got home, I couldn't walk." I wasn't affected by the activity to that degree after my first day, so I thought I was doing well compared to other people.

At times, the state would specify for rocks to be laid in a drainage area to prevent erosion. For one project, a grader notched out a 25-foot-wide area 300 feet long. We rolled out black filter cloth designed to prevent weed growth in this area. The next step was to place rock. The rock was brought up in a loader bucket. The smallest rocks permitted were softball sized. The largest were as large as you could carry. The loader bucket would be placed at waist height, and we would each carry rocks one at a time and place them. I was surprised how big a rock I could carry if I didn't need to pick it up off the ground. There were three of us working on this project, and we completed it in one day.

The Dog and the Dodge

On Saturdays, Beth and I would go on bike rides. Years before, she had taken a job cleaning a bank and she had been paid with 50-cent pieces. She had saved these and had purchased a Schwinn Continental the same summer I did as a kid, so we were evenly matched when it came to bikes. One day we were riding on the outskirts of town, heading out into the country, when we heard a dog barking. The dog had seen us coming and was running toward the road. From the direction he was heading, it appeared he wanted to position himself on the road in front of us when we got to him. He was a big dog. He had come off a porch and had 75 yards in which to build speed. We sped up to get ahead of him.

That dog never slowed down and never veered from his trajectory! He put his huge head right into the bottom bracket of my bike. When he hit me, everything went into slow motion. I remember sliding down the pavement and watching my bike flip over several times. It landed on the tires every time and then landed on the grass. I don't think it got a scratch.

With things still in slow motion, I saw a shadow coming over my head and heard a squealing sound. When everything settled down, my head was under the front bumper of a Dodge Volare. If I had a wrench, I could have reached out and loosened the drain plug on the engine's oil pan. The driver was shook up, thinking he had run me over. As he was getting out of his car, I was getting up off the road. He was relieved to see that I was alive. Meanwhile, the dog was yelping and running back to its house. The dog's owner came to the front door and yelled, "What did you do to my dog?"

I had torn the skin off my elbow in the incident. Beth wrapped my elbow up with a bandana, and we slowly rode back home. Once there, she washed the road grime out of the wound and bandaged me up. I could tell she was going to be a good nurse.

The Sunset Proposal

In late summer, I visited a jewelry store the father of a college classmate owned. I looked at rings, and he gave me a discount because I was a friend of his son. So naturally, I spent more than I had intended on a bigger diamond.

As I mentioned earlier, very early in our relationship Beth and

I knew we would be sticking together. In the months following our first few dates, it was quite common for us to have a conversation using the phrase "after we're married." Because of this, I wanted to make sure officially proposing and giving her the diamond would be a memorable occasion.

In September, I took Beth to Holland State Park on Lake Michigan. The beach was deserted. The sky was overcast. A lone sailboat was coming in from Lake Michigan with sails furled. Its mast was silhouetted by the yellow rays of the setting sun. We walked out on the pier. I stopped, turned to her, and proposed. She said *yes*, and I put the ring on her finger. She held out her hand and stared at the ring. In that moment, her realization that time would pass and we eventually would be married made her feel special.

However, we decided not to get married until after we both finished school. That date was almost two years away. To us, it looked like forever. There was also a challenge just around the corner that would threaten to take the dream away.

8

Grim Tales and a Fairy Tale

When I returned to college in the fall, one day I was browsing used paperback books in a bookstore and noticed a copy of a book titled *Eric*, written by his mother, Doris Lund. This was one of several non-fiction books from the 1970s that documented similar stories: A person in the prime of life would be diagnosed with cancer, and the book would follow the person's resulting heroic struggle for survival, including his or her ultimate demise.

This particular book had been made into a television movie. I had watched it when it first aired in 1975. What had impressed me then was how short life can be and how deeply having a life-threatening disease affects a person's view of life. I bought the book and read it. The book covered the time span from Eric being diagnosed the summer after he graduated from high school to his death at twenty-two years old. At the time, I was the same age as the main character in the book when he was in the midst of his struggle. Reading the book, the impact of dealing with a life-threatening situation hit home for me even more than when I had seen the movie. I didn't realize at the time, of course, how close I would soon come to dealing with the same kind of situation firsthand.

Academically it was my last year of college, and it went smoothly. One of the best classes I ever took was a course on how to conduct scientific studies and write scientific papers. The course was centered around ecology, and we would reenact historical studies to learn about the methods used in the past. One study I took part in involved sand dune blowouts along Lake Michigan. Beth and I have gone back to that beautiful location where the study took place many times over the years, to play in the waves and take in the beauty of that secluded stretch of coast.

My main paper for senior year blended my interest in road work and science. I did the paper on the impact of road salt runoff on aquatic life. Specifically, the effect on *Daphnia magna*, a small, transparent water bug. I found a journal documenting salt levels in road water runoff, so I had that part of the puzzle. Michigan State University's library contained a book on the species I was studying. Beth and I drove to East Lansing one Saturday so I could reference the book. It was a beautiful fall day. We could hear the roar from the football stadium as we walked to the library.

Deep in the recesses of the library building, on a shelf at floor level, we found the book, which had been published in the 1800s. The book documented that this species I was studying fed on plankton that filtered red light. The daphnia swam toward red light to find food. I raised these creatures in different levels of salt water and then tested their ability to react to red light. I found that high salt concentrations would affect the bugs' sense of the light, but not at the water runoff levels. My professor said if I went on to graduate school, my project would be a viable base on which to build. I didn't see graduate school as something I wanted to pursue, however, if I didn't have a specific goal in mind.

Beth's Academic Ordeal

For her last two years of nursing school, Beth lived with two classmates in the upstairs of an old house a few blocks from the hospital. One day I went to see her after she got out of class, and I found she was late coming back home. I went out to the sidewalk to see if she was coming. I could see her several houses away. She was dragging her backpack dejectedly. She ran up to me, and I could tell she was upset. I asked her what was wrong. She told me her instructor was going to throw her out of nursing school because she was unable to answer one specific question about the biliary system (the part of the "accessory" digestive tract that includes the gall bladder). Beth had asked for one more day to prepare. Her instructor told her that it would be her last chance.

I gave her a hug, and then we studied the biliary system that night! I looked over her course material and we reviewed it together. Then I quizzed her, and it sure looked to me as though she had mastered the material. The next day, Beth told her instructor she was ready for more questions. Her instructor broke down and cried. She apologized for what had happened the day before. She told Beth that she was dealing with serious personal issues and had let the issues get in the way. She never even asked Beth any follow-up questions. Looking back now, it is ironic that Beth has spent most of her nursing career as a digestive disease nurse.

New X-Rays, Old Story?

I graduated in the spring of 1982 with a Bachelor of Science degree focused on biology and chemistry. Jobs were hard to find that summer. I got out the old model M John Deere and put in another pickle patch. Then I put an ad in the newspaper to sell canning pickles to earn some gas money. It was frustrating not having a definite sense of direction when it came to work. In the fall, I applied for a laboratory position at a major food-processing company. The position was awarded to another applicant. I was told there were production line jobs available instead. I accepted.

Part of the hiring process at the company included being evaluated by an industrial doctor. The doctor was concerned about me lifting things with my spinal curvature. He had an X-ray taken of my back. When the X-ray was taken, however, the technician aimed the aperture lower than normal. The doctor noticed that near the bottom of the X-ray there was a cyst along the neck of my left femur, in the area that had been irradiated with the cobalt 60 when I was a baby.

I was allowed to hire in at the company with a weight restriction on my lifting, and I was also referred to an orthopedic doctor to follow up on the cyst. Dr. Andre had retired by then, and his practice had been taken over by Dr. Bukrey. I had already been seeing Dr. Bukrey annually for X-rays and follow-up for my back. When he heard about what the industrial doctor had spotted farther down, along my femur, he ordered more X-rays from a variety of angles. The result was that surgery was scheduled to deal with the cyst.

I checked into the hospital one Sunday evening, in preparation for surgery the next day. Dr. Bukrey came into my hospital room and said, "The X-rays were inconclusive. We need to do more tests before we do surgery." He explained that it was necessary to determine whether or not the cyst was attached to the bone. If it was attached, that could mean bone cancer.

I was discharged without surgery and came back to the hospital several days later for a bone scan. To prepare for a bone scan in those days, you drank a solution containing material that would bind to your bones and give off energy that could be picked up by a scanner. What the doctors were looking for were "hot spots."

I laid on the table and watched my skeleton on the monitor as my body was scanned. I could see my spinal curvature. I was shown the scan afterward and commented to the person showing me, "It looks like something is there." Facing the possibility of cancer was not as scary to me as it should have been, because deep down I never had a sense that if it turned out to be cancer, it would actually defeat me. Yet strangely enough, I really didn't turn to God fully at that point.

"Marry Him!"

The official report came back that there was activity in the area of the cyst, but not enough to be conclusive. Dr. Bukrey decided to go ahead with surgery, which was scheduled a few weeks away, in January. While this was going on, Beth was in her final year of nursing school.

This was when she was doing her pediatric rotation. She had gotten to know Dr. Johns and had found him to have the same fatherly "it's going to be all right" manner that I was so familiar with. My medical situation was burdening her. She stopped by his office one day to talk to him about it. Our wedding was planned for June 11. She told him what was going on and asked, "Should we postpone the wedding?"

Dr. Johns said only two words in reply: "Marry him!"

I was feeling a lot of frustration at this time. I was planning on getting married, with both the uncertainty of a diagnosis and the uncertainty of what to do for a career looming over my head. In my mind, I was the kid at the back of the bus all over again, being bounced around at every corner on an extremely bumpy ride while God, the cosmic bus driver, ignored what was going on behind Him. Nothing was going smoothly.

For example, a friend and I were planning on developing a soundproof enclosure for loud computer printers. I was working on a prototype in the basement. At one point, I got very frustrated when what I was attempting failed. I threw a tool into the corner. Everything going on right then just seemed to confirm the personal theology I had developed in high school, that God was almighty, but that He had shortchanged me in this life for some reason of His own. Big issues would frustrate me, and I wouldn't understand why I had to deal with such things when other people did not. But I still knew that somehow, God would bring me through them. I now believe that my understanding of God's love and protection—which I had in my spirit from the time I learned at three and four years old about God and what He had done for me as a baby—was still there in the background.

Beth and I met with the pastor of our church as all this was going on. At one point he made the statement to Beth, "For you, this could be the equivalent of widowhood." I believe he stated this to point out the seriousness of what we were dealing with and to encourage us to turn to God fully. My view of God as the uncaring bus driver was quite entrenched, however, so I still didn't fully give my concerns to Him at this point.

Giving It to God

The evening before the surgery, I was sitting in bed in my hospital room. My parents came in, Beth was there, and the pastor of our church also came in to pray with me. When visiting hours were over, I was by myself in bed. It was very dim in the room. Dr. Bukrey had stopped to see me earlier and had left a sleeping pill in case I needed it. It was on the table. A little light came in under the door. It was a bit chilly under the thin hospital blanket. The only sound was a faint hum from the heating system. At that point, it was between God and me. Surgery was scheduled for early the next morning.

Somehow, I knew I would come out the other side. The unknown of the next step is what weighed on me the most. I ended up giving it to God that night before surgery, alone in my hospital bed, yet not really in the best manner. It was as though I was saying, *Well, God, if this is what You planned for me, take me through it.*

The morning of surgery, the head elder of our church appeared at the hospital. He had told me once that at one point in his life he had two young children, was attempting to start a business, and had to have surgery. The surgery put him on his back for several months of recovery. He was now in his late fifties, his business was successful, and he employed many people. He wasn't even the elder assigned to me. He just took time out of his schedule and came out of concern. He prayed with me for a few minutes before I was taken into surgery.

The surgery went well. Dr. Bukrey reported that the cyst turned out to be one millimeter from my bone. Several days later, I got a phone call from the doctor's office. I was told the cyst was so obviously benign that the biopsy was only sent to one laboratory for confirmation. I had a strange response to the news. I wasn't excited. My attitude was more like, *Okay, we made it through that, so what happens from here?*

At a checkup after the ordeal, Dr Bukrey told me that the hospital was a teaching hospital. Challenging cases were reviewed each week by teams of doctors, residents, and interns. Prior to my surgery, the majority of the medical people attending those reviews thought my case would turn out to be bone cancer.

Beth graduated from nursing school in June 1983, a dream come true for her. She accepted a job working in the infectious disease isolation unit in the same hospital that had provided her schooling. Another job for me opened up in the lab at work. I would start the new job in the middle of June. Yet these successful steps in building our careers were about to be eclipsed by an even bigger event in our lives.

A Fairy-Tale Wedding

June 11, 1983, was our wedding day—a dream come true for both of us. Just prior to Beth and me stating our wedding vows, our pastor presented the following thoughts on marriage:

> Steve and Beth, we have chosen for your wedding meditation the brief words of Philippians 4:4–7 [ASV]. These words: "Rejoice in the Lord always: again I will say, Rejoice. Let your forbearance be known unto all men. The Lord is at hand. In nothing be anxious; but in everything by prayer and supplication with thanksgiving let your requests be made known unto God. And the peace of God, which passeth all understanding, shall guard your hearts and your thoughts in Christ Jesus."
>
> We have here in this text a perfect plan of God for your lives. And, if you use this plan, in your marriage, it will become such a formative plan for your lives the result of which would be, if you follow this order, your marriage in quality will far surpass 99 percent of all the other marriages around you. In this text there are four parts. Four ingredients that you have to put into your marriage.
>
> They are power, patience, prayer, and peace.
>
> The first ingredient is power. Listen. "Rejoice in the Lord always: again I will say, rejoice." Maybe it seems a little bit silly or a little bit unnecessary to even tell you to here at your wedding ceremony that you are supposed to rejoice. Rejoice! Oh, keep in mind

here that many people rejoice in things. They rejoice in people, or in circumstances. But listen to the words carefully: *Rejoice in the Lord.* Some people put their joy in things—people, and circumstances, and cars, or the houses they bought. Or a nice bride or a top-notch, first-class husband. Don't put your joy today in each other or in things or in circumstances, but anchor your joy in the Lord.

The word *Lord* means owner. He owns you. The Lord Jesus owns you. He bought you with His blood on the cross at Calvary. Therefore, if you rejoice in Him, your joy will be solid, your joy will be eternal, your life will be filled with power because He is eternal and He is powerful. Joy in the Lord, that's your power.

The second ingredient is patience: "Let your forbearance be made known unto all men. The Lord is at hand." The word *forbearance* means patience. And everybody knows that a marriage needs patience. And you are going to need it too. The word *patience* in forbearance means extra special, extra kind, extra loving patience. Use that toward each other. Patience. Every good marriage needs it. If you practice this kind of extra special, extra kind, extra tender patience to each other and put that ingredient in your marriage, this text guarantees you will never have an argument! It is impossible to get mad at someone who is always loving kind and patient. They are too nice. You can be patient because the Lord is at hand. The Lord is nearby. The Lord is in your hearts; He is in your home. If the Lord is in your home, He controls everything. If the Lord takes care of every single detail of your life, every day, every hour, every year, every decade, what's there to get uptight about? What's there to be impatient about? Be patient—the Lord is at hand.

A third ingredient. Put in your marriage prayer. Listen: "In nothing be anxious; but in everything by prayer and supplication with thanksgiving let your requests be made known unto God." *In nothing be anxious.* Never be anxious. Don't let anxiousness creep into your lifestyle. It only fills the human life with worry, tension, headaches, and ulcers. In nothing be anxious, but in everything use prayer to place it in God's hands. Use the prayer as a tool, to take the good times and the bad times, the special joyous occasions like this, but also the sad and sober occasions, place them in the Lord's hands. You already know that prayer works. The two of you already know many things about prayer. Last January when the two of you were awaiting the outcome of a surgery, you found out many things about prayer. Prayer is a tool. It's a tool whereby we can take life's burdens from our shoulders and put them on the Lord's shoulders.

There are three kinds of prayer: ordinary prayer, supplication, and thanksgiving. Ordinary prayer, yes, every day. Supplication is earnest, pleading, "when you really mean it prayer," and thanksgiving is joyous, happy prayer. Use all three as tools to take your life's concerns and put them in the Lord's hands.

And one more ingredient—the last one is peace: "... and the peace of God which passeth all understanding shall guard your hearts and thoughts in Christ Jesus." Peace, that's what you want, right? If you know that God controls all things, if you know that He is taking care of every detail so not a hair can fall from your head, nothing can happen, everything in your entire life, for the rest of your life, is totally in His control. If you really know that, and really believe that deep inside, then there comes a solid peace out of that, a peace so stable nothing can shake you, because peace is far better than knowledge or understanding. It's much better to have God's peace by you day by day than for the two of you to know what all is going to happen between now and the year 2030. God's peace shall guard your hearts and thoughts in Christ Jesus. That's the bottom line, in Christ.

In your marriage, strive to please Christ. If people try to please themselves they only grow discontent and sour. If you try to please each other, as many people try in marriage, they only grow after a while bored, sad. Try to please Christ, and His peace will guard your hearts and souls. Please Him, and this guarantees that His power, patience, prayer, and peace will all come together in His perfect plan for your marriage, and your marriage will be in quality far surpassing all those other marriages around you. That's Gods plan.

After the wedding reception, Beth and I drove romantically into the sunset for a honeymoon on the Lake Michigan coastline. On the drive, Beth looked at my wedding ring and thought, *We are actually married for the rest of our lives!* It was like a fairy-tale ending to that challenging chapter in our lives.

9

Blazing Trails as Newlyweds

After our honeymoon, we settled into the same upstairs apartment in the same house that Beth had lived in with her roommates when she had gone to nursing school. The house had definitely seen better days, but as newlyweds we didn't care. We were starting a whole new life together.

Given the experience we went through just before we were married, with all the unknown circumstances surrounding my surgery, you'd think we would have found it easy to live out the principles the pastor presented to us in our wedding meditation. Especially when minor issues would pop up. Yet I can testify that just because God has done a lot for people, it doesn't automatically make them line up with how He would have them behave. As a young husband, I was a prime example of that.

Take showing my wife loving patience. One day soon after our honeymoon, Beth was making breakfast and she cracked open an egg that turned out to be rotten. She proceeded to crack open a second egg to see if it was the same. It was. As she went to crack open a third, I said, "Why in the world would you keep cracking open rotten eggs and smelling up the place?!" Her response was that she wanted to see if they were all that way. My response was, "That makes no sense! You won't be using any of that dozen, so why would you want to open them all up?"

Beth took my response as questioning her intelligence. It really hurt her feelings, when her intent simply had been to satisfy her curiosity about whether all the eggs were affected. She had no intention of eating any of them. So much for my having patience. I had to learn to look beyond the immediate frustration of little things going wrong in life and instead look at the big picture. I am still not always successful in doing that!

Within a month of us moving in, the landlords announced that they were selling the house and we would have to move out. When my dad came over to help us, he commented, "I don't know how anyone could accumulate so much stuff in a month!" We found another apartment on the ground floor of a four-unit building and settled in—again.

Settling into our jobs was even more of a challenge. Starting out in the work world meant being scheduled for less than ideal work hours. I was working second shift. Beth was rotating days and nights, putting in eight-hour shifts that would include two out of three weekends. With some of her days off essentially being sleep days for her, we would see each other for a few minutes when we would come and go, as well as on Wednesday mornings and every third weekend.

Hiking into Adventure

With all that going on, we still found opportunity for some adventure. In my new job, I had an extra week of vacation I needed to use before the end of the year. Beth managed to rearrange her hours one week to get Monday through Friday off. I picked her up at the hospital after her Sunday night shift, and we headed south. Our first destination was Cumberland Falls State Resort Park in Kentucky. We checked into the campground on a misty, dark evening. The attendant told us, "If you don't want to cook in the rain, you can go to the CCC [Civilian Conservation Corps] lodge for dinner."

We thought that sounded like a great idea, so after we put up our borrowed tent we went to the lodge and enjoyed the food and the rustic architecture. On the way back to the campground, we saw a sign with an arrow that said *Falls Parking*. We turned in. The lights were off in the back end of the deep, narrow parking lot. We parked near the entrance and found some steps that led to a natural, uneven stone surface that stretched into the darkness. We walked down the steps, and as we went farther into the darkness we could hear the roar of the waterfall.

As the noise of the rushing water increased, Beth asked, "Where is it?"

I responded, "As loud as it is, it has to be above us and right in front of us."

Our eyes started to adjust, and we took a few more tentative steps ahead. Suddenly, we saw water rushing from left to right just inches from our feet. When I looked a couple of feet to my right, I could see white water, and beyond it nothing but a void. We knew that didn't look good, so we retreated. On the way back, I noticed a post and a cable. When we returned the next morning, we could clearly see that the post and cable were supposed to keep people out of the danger zone. In the dark we had not seen this barrier and had walked past it—right up to the side of the stream. We had been standing at the very edge of the top of the falls!

We continued on to spend a couple of days in the Great Smoky Mountain National Park. The weather was spectacular, with colors in full bloom. In fact, a park ranger told us that the sky was unusually clear that year, the rainfall patterns during the spring and summer were ideal for color formation in the leaves, and as a result we were experiencing what could be a once-in-a-lifetime nature show! We made it back home in time for me to drop Beth off for a night shift on Friday night.

Having grown up on a bit of farmland, to me our apartment felt confining. During the snowy winter being in a snug apartment was not so bad, but in the spring the urge to get out and have some adventure hit repeatedly. We had spoken with people who had been to Rocky Mountain National Park, and it inspired us to visit there for some backpacking. We spent our time off that summer preparing for the big trip. We purchased a new tent, along with backpacks, a cooking kit, big, bulky hiking shoes, and miscellaneous camping gear. We studied up on what to pack and how to prepare for such an outing.

We even took some practice hikes. One Saturday, we went to a wilderness area with sand dunes along Lake Michigan. We wanted to get in some time hiking with full backpacks, so we went into the dunes and eventually got lost. After a while I told Beth, "If we walk west, we'll come to the lake."

Up and over the dunes we went. When we found the lake, we were much farther from the car than we thought. We had quite a hike left even after our hike! The exercise was quite taxing on my body, causing me musculoskeletal pain afterward. In the midst of these preparations for our trip, the 1984 Olympics was taking place. One of my schoolmates from high school, who had participated in that track club meet where I took the shortcut I told you about, won a bronze medal in the steeplechase. My thought about that was, *Good for him. God gives him what it takes to go to the Olympics and win a medal, and I can't hike with a backpack without paying for it.* It made me all the more determined to go to Colorado and climb a mountain.

So a Bear Walks By . . .

In late August, Beth and I packed all our gear into our brown 1982 Datsun hatchback and headed out West. We spent the first night in a small town in Nebraska. We arrived at dusk, driving by big grain elevators on the way in. It was a warm Friday night, and we could see the local high school football team on the brightly lit field. We ate at McDonald's. An old farmer came in wearing a red plaid shirt, jeans, suspenders and a red Dekalb corn cap. The help was talking about how packed the place would be after the game. It was a real slice of America's heartland.

The next day, we continued driving across the plains. In the early afternoon mountains came into view. We arrived at Rocky Mountain National Park and went to the backcountry office to ask what backcountry sites were available the next night. The attendant told us most sites were taken, but no one had reserved the Fern Lake site for the next night. I told them we would take it. The attendant made the statement, "There's bear activity in that area."

I thought, *So a bear walks by* . . . Beth didn't say anything, and we obtained the backcountry permit. We pitched our tent in a developed campground in the park for the first night and got some rest. The next morning, we drove to the trailhead and got out our gear. We strapped our tent and sleeping bags to our already prepacked backpacks, put on our bandanas, and got going. We headed up the trail to the Fern Lake campsite—a trail that was 3½ miles long and gained 1400 feet in elevation. Every four feet we moved forward, we went up a foot. It was like climbing stairs. The rocky path was also uneven. Each time we took a stride, it was a different length. Part way up, two people from the park service came up from behind us on mules. They asked where we were going, checked our backcountry permit, and said, "Have a good time!" Then they went on ahead of us.

The trail up was taxing on me, but I was proving to myself that I could do it and that I would not be denied doing what normal people could do. We arrived at the designated spot for our campsite and sized up the situation. The trail dead-ended into the campsite. There was a rope provided by the park service about 40 feet off to the side of the trail. It was strung 10 feet high between two trees on a small ridge. The rope was provided so we could hang our food up high to keep it away from bears. About 150 feet beyond the rope, at the very end of the trail, was a flat area to pitch the tent. We set up our tent and then set to work hanging up our backpacks and food sack. I had a nylon clothesline in my backpack. I tied our backpacks to this line and threw it over the park service rope. I then put a log up against another tree, climbed up, and tied off my rope horizontally, with the backpacks suspended high in the air. I then threw the excess rope over the park service line, hoisted our food sack up as well, and secured the line.

We then hiked to the lake to take in the beauty. And beautiful it was! Large mountains all around the lake, as well as large pines and ferns. When we returned to the campsite we prepared to make dinner. We took the food sack down, took out what we needed, and rehung the sack. The campsite was next to a steep ravine with a small stream flowing through it. We went down to the stream to cook in order to keep any food odors away from the tent. When we came to the top of the ravine after eating, our tent didn't look right. The front screen had been ripped open, and one of the aluminum tent poles had been bent. Beth said, "I think a raccoon was here!"

Seeing the damage, my response was, "I don't think that was a raccoon!"

We looked over to where the backpacks were hanging. There was a huge black bear sitting there. He had gotten our food sack down and was eating Pop-Tarts from our pack. *What do we do now?* I thought with some trepidation.

The trail into our campsite came through an area with a lot of rocks, boulders, brush, and downed tree limbs, and it dead-ended at our campsite. There was no trail to go farther down to get away from the bear. We decided we had to leave everything and get out of there by going back the direction we had come in. The challenge was that if we took the trail to leave, we would have to go right past the bear. That didn't look like a good option! We decided to go back down to the stream, follow the stream beyond the bear, come back up, find the trail, and get out.

We headed down the ravine and along the stream, which eventually veered away from the trail. Concerned that we wouldn't be able to find the trail again if we went farther downstream, we came back up the side of the ravine at that point and found ourselves right behind the bear. Retreat! We headed back down the ravine. I slipped going across the stream and dropped my only weapon, my jackknife. It is in that stream to this day. When we came up again, we ended up in front of our tent, right where we had started.

It was getting toward evening and we had been going in circles—one circle trying to avoid the bear and another circle taking us right back around to our tent and to him once again. Darkness was going to fall, so it seemed our only option was to walk past the bear.

We decided to grab what we would need to survive overnight, in case we got hurt somehow on the hike out—if we made it past the bear to begin with. Our sleeping bags were still in their stuff sacks in the tent. We took those and put a canteen in each one, along with our map, a compass, and a signal mirror. We had no food because the bear had our food sack.

As we were preparing to make our exit, the bear got up and started pacing back and forth under the park service rope. We didn't dare walk past him at that point. We just stood there. After a bit, the bear went to one of the trees holding up the rope, stood up on his back paws, put his front paws on the tree, and one, two, three, climbed up to the level of the park service rope. The bear hung on the tree with his left paw and reached out to our backpacks with his right paw. He was leaning out so far that I could see light between his body and the tree.

We decided it was time to walk past him, while he was preoccupied up the tree. The trail passed 40 feet from the bear. With the surrounding brush, I didn't want to take a detour off the trail and make any noise. We started down the trail toward the bear. He could barely reach our backpacks. He was hitting them on the frames with his paw and had them spinning.

When we were even with the bear, he noticed us and snapped his head in our direction. We froze. Beth started silently saying the Lord's Prayer. The bear started coming down. After climbing halfway down he stopped and hung there, looking at us. After what seemed like hours, he climbed back up. We hurried down the trail. The last we heard from the bear was the sound of crashing branches as he kept going after our backpacks.

It was getting close to sunset. In the Rockies sunset is like *boom, out-go-the-lights* if you are in the shadow of the mountain. Fortunately, most of the trail back was in a valley with an east-to-west orientation. Uneven, steep, rocky trails, we found out, were actually more difficult to navigate going downhill than up. The sun was setting, and the rocks along the trail were casting long shadows. It was just getting totally dark when we reached the trailhead. A ranger was there helping two little old ladies jump-start their car. We told him what had happened with the bear.

"It's been quite a night," the ranger replied. "We had a Big Foot reported in the zone north of here." He went on to tell us, "The park service has been tracking that bear. We estimate that it weighs three hundred pounds." He said before our adventure a man had been camping on the same site by himself in an open-ended tent. In the middle of the night he had his arm sticking out of the tent, and he woke up when the bear was licking his arm. He pulled his arm inside, lay in the tent until daylight, and ran down the mountain.

The mounted park service people we had interacted with on our climb up were retrieving his camping gear for him. The same people also retrieved our gear. They told us we had done everything right. The backpack company even repaired one backpack for us and sent us a new one under the warranty. The more heavily damaged one they retained. It was put on display at their headquarters!

Setting Sail Closer to Home

The next spring, Beth and I started looking for a house. We had been saving money, and we had a good down payment. We found a three-bedroom ranch at a reasonable price. This was a new kind of adventure for us.

We did the usual painting of our new place. It turns out that painting ceilings requires a lot of stretching overhead and twisting. I did well while we were in the process, but I was frustrated afterword, when I experienced musculoskeletal pain that lasted several days as a result.

My frustrations with such limitations were counterbalanced with learning some new skills and making use of them. Beth unintentionally taught me to sail on Tamarack Lake, a small lake in the town of Lakeview where she grew up. She took me out in the fourteen-foot Porpoise sailboat her parents had purchased many years before, and she ran the boat into the reeds at the edge of the lake. When she jumped out to turn the boat around, the wind caught the sail with me on the boat by myself! I quickly learned to sail and managed to sail back to her and pick her up.

For recreation that summer, we would take the Porpoise to Gun

Lake. This large lake has many long bays going off in various directions—an ideal arrangement for finding a favorable angle of wind in which to play with a small sailboat. We enjoyed many hours of ideal sailing conditions on Gun Lake. When we weren't setting sail, we settled into our house and into a routine.

10

Reaching Out

About a year after Beth and I were married, I started exploring the possibilities of what could be done for the aftereffects of my early medical treatment. I went to a physical therapist to deal with the tension in my musculoskeletal system. The exercises the therapist gave me did very little for me. I then started digging into whatever information I could find on what to expect for my medical future. I found out that before I was born so few people had survived a Wilms tumor that there was no data on what survivors my age could expect long-term.

The National Wilms Tumor Study that began in 1969, and which I talked about in chapter 4, was continuing to record information on current cases of Wilms tumors as they came up. The purpose of the study was to track the survival rates of patients as new treatments were being developed and to monitor long-term side effects. It took a national study with many hospitals participating to generate significant data since so few cases came up each year. Of course, the people in this study were treated at least nine years after I was, so the data being gathered on them would help future patients. With the time lag and treatment shifting from cobalt 60 to chemotherapy, however, the data did very little to answer my question.

Since the study had little data to offer me, I wrote to a couple of well-known medical centers that deal with childhood cancer and asked for any information related to my concern. I was sent some written information with scary predictions of a significant increase in the risk of various types of cancer. I made the decision that I was not going to live in fear and filed these papers away.

Soon after this, a young man from our church was diagnosed with Ewing sarcoma, a type of bone cancer. This was considered a pediatric disease, but he was in his early twenties. His mother had joined the congregation a few years earlier. She had been a widow for several years. This young man would come to church with his mother, and they would leave right after the service. He hadn't gotten involved with any young-adult activities the way Beth and I had, so I hadn't gotten to know him.

Over the next many months, we would not see him in church much. When we did, you could see the effects of his cancer treatment. He was almost bald and was getting thin. From time to time there would be an announcement on how he was doing. When I heard these announcements, I would really feel for him in my heart, but I didn't know what I would say to him to encourage him. The doctors had him on several courses of different chemotherapy drugs. Eventually, he had a metastasis with several spots in his lungs. The doctors didn't have a straightforward plan for him. It was announced that he was going to be part of a research program at the National Institutes of Health (NIH) in Washington, D.C.

Something Churning in Me

I read the book *Eric* again and was reminded of what people going through cancer treatment deal with. I knew this young man was going through treatment at a very large specialty cancer hospital similar to the one described in the book. I was also beginning to feel I should reach out to him. I wasn't sure what I really had to offer or exactly why I was feeling compelled to interact with him. One thing I knew, however—something was churning in me.

One summer day I called his house. His mother answered the phone. When she passed the phone to him, I heard her say, "It's someone from church."

I thought, *What do I say now?* When the young man said hello,

I said, "Hi, my name is Steve. Do you remember me?" He said he thought he remembered me. I asked him how he was doing, and he answered that the normal chemotherapy drugs had not worked for him. He told me he was part of a new program that meant he would be in Washington for a few weeks at a time to get trial chemotherapy drugs. He would return home for several weeks of recovery afterward, and then he would go back to Washington for another round. He would be leaving for the next treatment in a week. He invited me to come by the house to see him.

I drove to his house a couple of days later. I had not seen him at church for many months. He was growing his hair back after his last round of chemotherapy. I knew our pastor would visit him, but other than that, I could sense that he didn't really have people beyond his mother to talk to about what he was going through. I told him about my history of having a Wilms tumor and about the later cyst near my femur. He shared with me some details about his own history—how two of the cancer spots in his lung had gone away, what drugs had been tried, and the history of the trial drug he was being given at NIH.

This began a series of visits I made to this young man when he was home. At one point, NIH allowed him to have the chemotherapy locally. I would travel downtown to see him in the hospital. One time I took a pocket Bible with me, intending to share a psalm with him when I saw him. I never took it out of my pocket. We just got talking. He reflected on his lung tumors going away. He recognized that God had a hand in that.

In the fall of 1985, Beth and I went on another vacation to the Smoky Mountains in Tennessee. The young man from church was at NIH at the time. He was on the last trial drug that had any history of human use. He was expecting results soon. The weather turned rainy in Tennessee, so we decided to drive to Cape Hatteras, North Carolina, to see the ocean. I was thinking we could stop by Washington on the way home from North Carolina and see him. I called NIH from the campground pay phone to find out how long he would be in Washington. The hospital operator put me through to him. He said it would work for us to stop and see him. A week later, we arrived in Washington and got a hotel.

The next morning, we went to the NIH building where he was being treated. It was a very tall, large building. One thing I vividly remember is the area in front of the elevators. It was a simple, large open area servicing banks of four elevators on both sides of the walkway. Seeing this large space and the many elevators really opened my eyes to how many people were receiving treatment here. We took the elevator up and went to the Ewing sarcoma ward. This was a rare disease, and NIH was an international treatment center. Many other patients with the same condition occupied the ward. They all had bald heads. Several were dealing with dry heaves, a side effect of the chemotherapy.

We found my friend, who looked as if he had lost a significant amount of weight. He had also lost quite a bit of strength. I could tell he was struggling. I knew he appreciated the visit, but he was not up to much interaction that day. After he returned home, he received a report that the drug he was on when Beth and I saw him at NIH had not worked for him. They told him the last option was a drug that had only been tried on animals. He decided that he had gone through enough suffering from chemotherapy drugs and was not going to go that route.

Now that he was home for good, I visited him several more times. I was concerned about the fact that the doctors were saying it was just a matter of time before he passed away. He had not become a member of the church, but what concerned me most of all was that in all our interactions he had mentioned God just a couple of times. I knew he had long hours during his stays at NIH and during his recovery times at home to contemplate his situation. I knew he recognized that the lung spots disappearing was an act of God. I also knew that he was facing a terminal disease with no medical hope, and he was wondering why things were going that way.

One night after the evening church service, I was talking with our pastor about my concern as we walked to the parsonage. As he opened the door, I said to him, "I really don't know what to do. I wish I had been to seminary."

Turning to look at me, with the wind whipping snowflakes in his hair, our pastor said, "They don't teach you how to handle situations like this in seminary." Then he went inside.

It's Over, Yet Eternal

At one point after a couple more visits, I decided just to be bold and ask the young man if he had accepted Jesus as his Savior. He said he had. A week later, I called to talk to him. His mother answered and told me, "It's over." He had passed away.

After my friend passed away, a mutual acquaintance asked me if the young man had told me about what had happened to him just before he left NIH for the last time. I said no. The young man had told our mutual acquaintance an account of getting out of the shower and having a vision of Jesus. Standing in the shower doorway, Jesus was telling him that he would soon know why things were taking place the way they were.

I was asked to be a pallbearer at his funeral. I lined up on the left side of the casket so I could lift from my right side, the side unaffected by the Wilms. We laid the young man to rest in the township cemetery next to his parents' plots. His headstone is a government-issue headstone with a cross on top and the dates *March 9, 1961 – December 6, 1985*. A U.S. flag flies next to the headstone. He had not served in the military, but rather had served his country by being a volunteer for the clinical testing of trial cancer drugs. I visit the grave at least once a year to brush the pine needles off the stone and remember someone who truly became a friend and brother.

A few years later, our pastor accepted a call to pastor at another church. Decades later, I crossed paths with him again. When we spoke, he told me that shortly before the young man had passed away, he had shared that all his friends had abandoned him when the going got rough and that I was the only person near his age that he considered a friend. The pastor told me that over the years since then, there were times when, without mentioning names, he would share our story in a sermon as an example of what the communion of the saints means.

I didn't consider doing what I had done with this young man exceptional, so I really didn't know what to say in response to the pastor's words. However, hearing those words did cause me to reflect. I realize now it had been God prompting me to reach out to that young man. Reaching out to him when he was in a life-and-death struggle had been uncomfortable for me, but the reward is an eternal friendship. I look forward to seeing him in heaven.

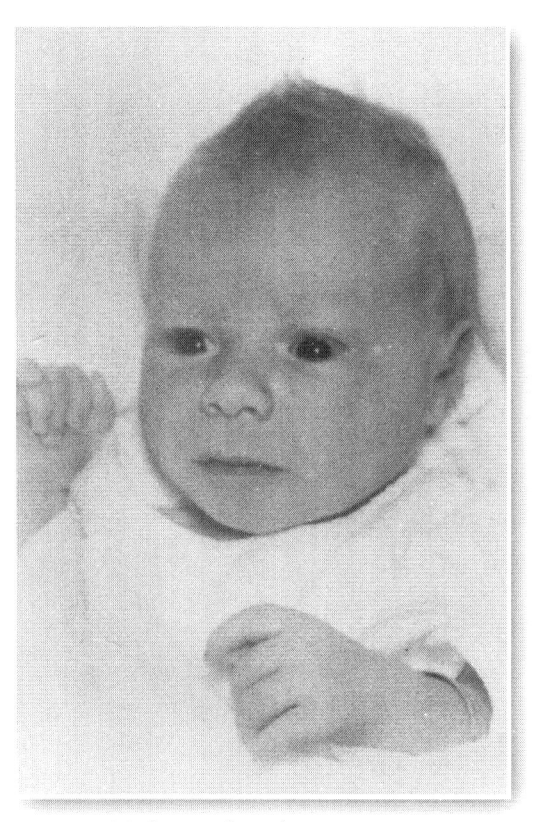

My hospital newborn picture.

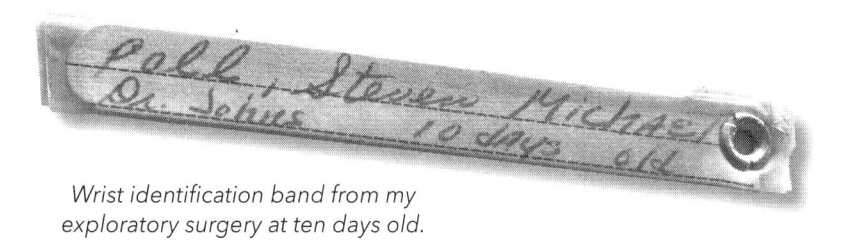

Wrist identification band from my exploratory surgery at ten days old.

Dad holding me on the day of my baptism, the day before my first cobalt treatment.

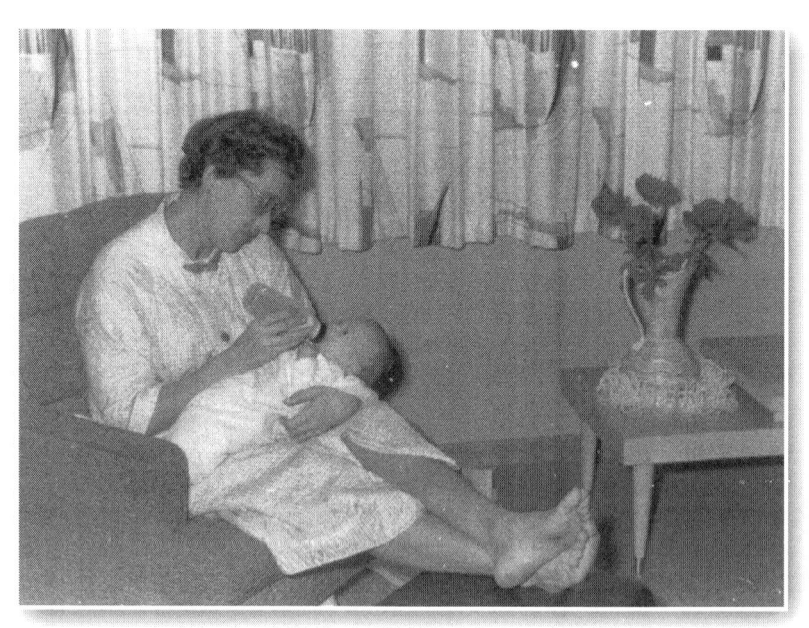

Mom giving me one of my frequent bottle feedings.

The NRX nuclear reactor. For many years, it was the only reactor powerful enough to create cobalt 60 used in treating deep-seated tumors. Courtesy of Toronto Public Library.

NO WEDGES:

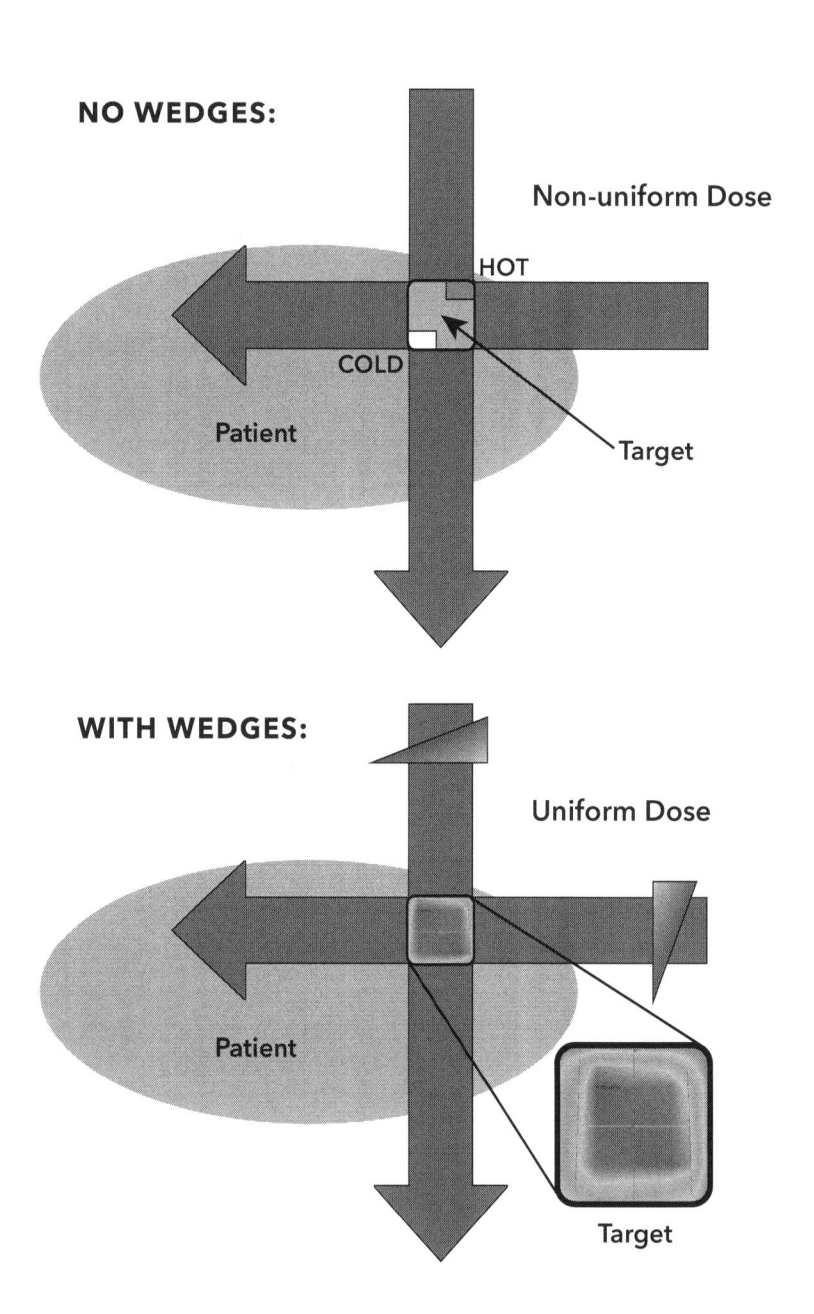

Non-uniform Dose

HOT
COLD
Patient
Target

WITH WEDGES:

Uniform Dose

Patient
Target

Illustration of the reason for using lead wedges in my cobalt 60 treatment plan. Courtesy of Dr. Jerry Battista, Ph.D., who also provided technical information on the design and historical use of the Theratron.

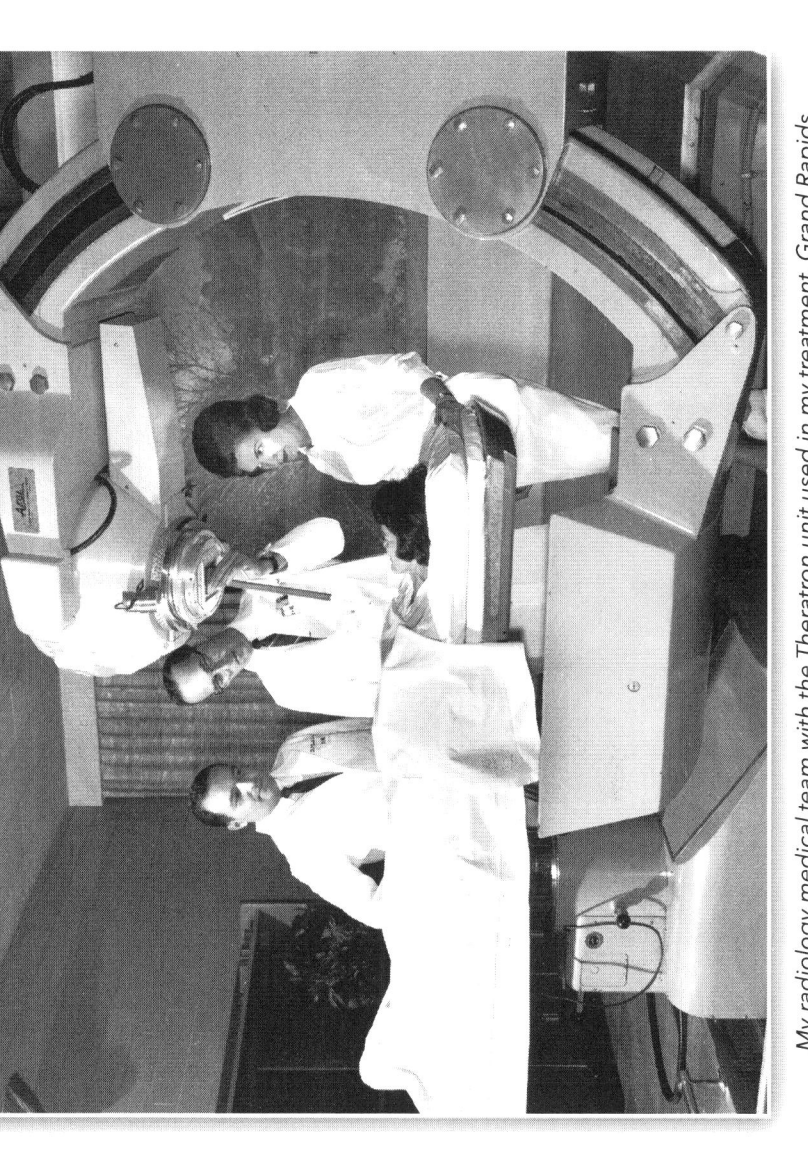

My radiology medical team with the Theratron unit used in my treatment. Grand Rapids History & Special Collections, Archives, Grand Rapids Public Library, Grand Rapids, MI.

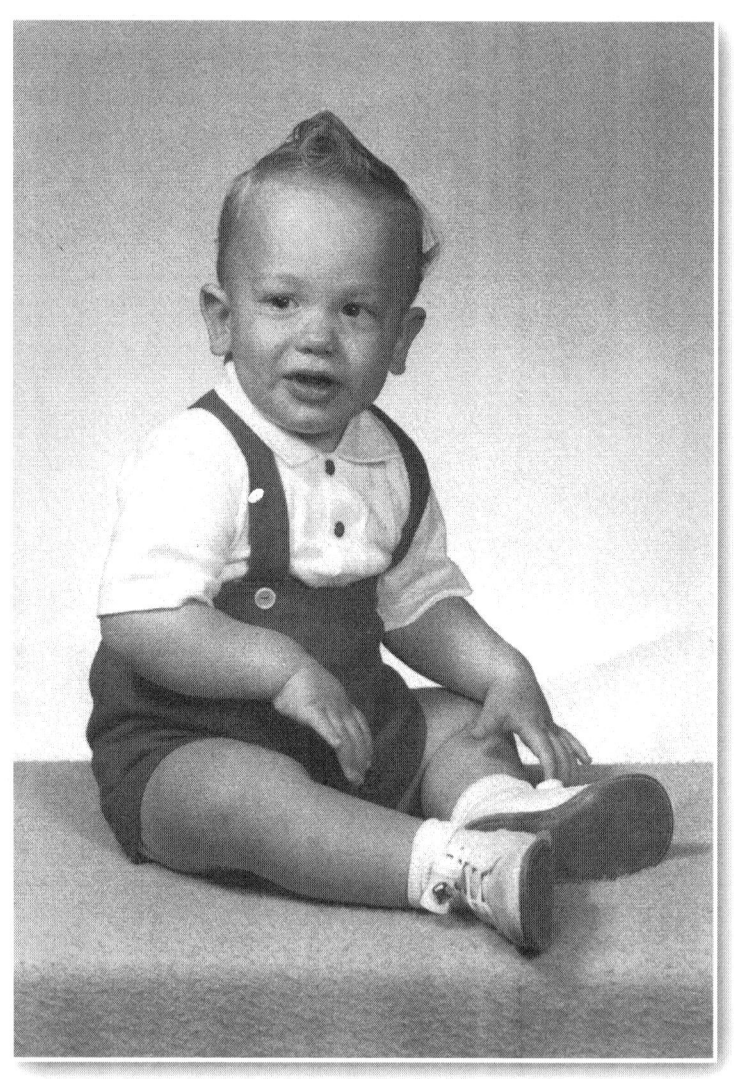

My six-month studio photograph.

In my soccer uniform my last year of junior high.

The two of us celebrating our engagement.

One of my favorite pictures of Beth, her nursing class photo.

Both photos: KVO Photography

The Fairytale wedding.

Me on the pier at Holland State Park with our girls. My spinal curvature and my left side's missing structure are noticeable even in a photograph.

Picture of our kids taken about the time Beth had her migraine pain lock in.

Our teardrop trailer.

Beth and me in our mid-fifties. Notice how my spine is now straight. (The zipper on my shirt actually lines up with my belt buckle!)

11

Filtered Theology and Starting a Family

I was unsettled about what I was doing in life. After my interactions with the terminally ill young man from church, I started wondering if I should become a pastor. I looked into what additional classes I would need to prepare myself for seminary. I started taking two of those classes, along with working full time.

During this time, a kind of odd possibility for a twist in our life direction came up. One morning, Beth cared for a patient who asked her if she had ever considered being a model. Beth was getting used to having patients ask odd personal questions and simply said no. Later, this patient said again, "Are you sure you wouldn't want to be a model? Models make a lot more money than nurses!"

Beth replied that she didn't want men gawking at her. The patient shrugged it off after that. When Beth went to lunch, she shared the interaction with two other nurses. They both stared at her, and one of them said, "Do you know who that patient is? One of the head executives at one of the top modeling agencies in the world!"

Beth came home and told me about the interaction, and we just looked at each other. I had always thought she looked as if she could be a model, so this didn't surprise me at all. The AIDS crisis was going on, and several of the nurses Beth worked with had been getting accidental needle sticks. They would then be tested for AIDS, and several of them were told to postpone having children until it was certain they had not become infected. Beth had been wondering if she wanted to continue in such a high-risk profession. It only took a few seconds to think through the situation. If you sign on as a model and don't make it, you are back where you started. If you sign on and they like you, it is likely that in a few years you will be replaced anyway. If you sign on and things go really well, it could be very hard on personal relationships. Beth decided that direct patient-care nursing was her true calling.

A few years later, the hospital Beth worked at merged with a smaller specialty hospital that was considered world-class in its field. Beth was assigned to work on the specialty unit. In addition to the local population, the hospital attracted the rich and famous from all across the country, as well as patients from other countries. I would eat lunch with Beth at the hospital on Sundays. For a few years, it wasn't surprising to walk down a hall on the unit she worked on and glance into a room with an open door, only to see a well-known, prominent person sitting in a chair. Beth's interaction with the modeling executive early in her career was one of several experiences that prepared her for dealing with various types of people. Over the years, she has taken care of patients from every segment of society. Among the many things she has learned firsthand about people is that we all have the same needs, and that there are times when people's status or wealth cannot gain for them the health or peace of mind they desire.

The Question of Sickness

I did very well in my seminary prep classes. In fact, my GPA was way higher in these courses than my final GPA when I graduated from college. One course I took was developmental psychology. I was getting all A's on the tests. One day the professor asked me to talk with him in his office. He said, "I know you're working and going to school. You older students coming back and getting all A's aren't getting much from driving in here and sitting in class. If you want, you can stop attending and promise me you'll finish reading the textbook. Then

11. FILTERED THEOLOGY AND STARTING A FAMILY

write a paper on a topic of your choice related to the course material. Just stop in to let me know what you are doing once in a while."

I decided to take him up on his offer. I shared my decision to take up the offer with another student, who said to me, "That might not have been a good idea. That professor offered the same option to a friend of mine who was getting an A, and he didn't do well on the paper. He was given a B in the class."

I had already committed to doing a paper, however, so I thought over possibilities for a topic. I chose to write my paper on why suffering occurs and God's role in the situation. I thought I was being objective as I wrote it. Yet while I was conducting my research, I was filtering my thoughts through my personal theology—the bus driver allegory I described for you earlier, where I had developed this idea that God was the bus driver and for some reason He had chosen to put me in the back of the bus, where I'd really feel the bumps on the ride to heaven.

Instead of turning directly to the Bible for my initial research, I consulted historical theology books written by men educated in the same religious tradition as the denomination I was raised in. My thought was, *These people have studied extensively, and their writings are highly respected. How far wrong can I go by starting with looking at what they taught?* First, I used some passages I found in their books to validate my personal viewpoint. Then I referenced Bible passages I also found that appeared to back up these traditional viewpoints.

I started the paper by making the observation that Christians come up with various responses to the question, *Why am I sick?* I noted that the range of responses includes lack of faith, or God struck you in this way because of a specific sin, or the devil did this to you because God would never bring evil upon anybody. Or, some Christians don't even see any supernatural activity being involved in a sickness; they simply give a scientific explanation of the disease and its natural causes.

I then set out to answer the following questions:

1. Why do sickness and pain exist?
2. Does sickness come from natural causes, the devil, or God?

3. What is the purpose of sickness and pain in the believer's life?
4. What is the proper response of the believer?

It was a lengthy paper. What follows here is a summary of my conclusions, which will show you show where I was at in my thinking when I did my research. As you will see, I was definitely filtering my thoughts through my own theology at the time.

When answering the first question concerning why sickness and pain exist, my observation was that suffering can be traced to the fall of Adam and Eve in the Garden of Eden. If they had not disobeyed God's command, death and its physical forerunners of sickness and pain would not exist (see Genesis 2:17).

My second question was, "Does sickness come from natural causes, the devil, or God?" To find an answer, I framed my thinking based on excerpts from the historical theological works I had located. Here is one example from Dutch theologian and statesman Abraham Kuyper: "... from moment to moment you are operated upon by your God, and that nothing overtakes you, *except what He brings upon you*."[2]

I then looked at many biblical accounts of sickness and death, all the way from Miriam and her leprosy in the Old Testament to the apostle Paul and his affliction of the flesh in the New Testament. Some biblical cases of sickness appeared to have a "natural cause," some were directly attributed to Satan, and in one case it is stated that an angel of the Lord struck down a person in judgment. I concluded that in every instance, in every case I looked at, God was ultimately in control of the situation and had not intervened, so He must have approved of what was going on.

The third question I set out to answer was, "What is the purpose of sickness and pain in the believer's life?" (In reality, I was asking if there was a reason I had been left to face challenges that others did not.) To answer this question, I again quoted Abraham Kuyper. His observation was that it takes more for God to get through to some of us than others. He said, "Driving nails into iron demands a firmer

---

2. Abraham Kuyper, *In the Shadow of Death*, trans. John Hendrik De Vries (Grand Rapids: Eerdmans, 1929), 29.

blow than driving nails into wainscot [wood] . . . the one must be struck far more forcefully than the other."[3]

Kuyper also addressed the question, "Why does who is afflicted appear unfair?" He wrote, "The question itself is already ungodly when it implies a finding fault with God's providential direction."[4] I also found a proverb that I thought explained why we should not question what happens: "The Lord works out everything for his own ends" (Proverbs 16:4 NIV 1984).

The fourth question I asked was, "What is the proper response of the believer?" My answer to this question was that we were supposed to seek God. I continued, however, by asking two additional questions: Can we expect to be restored to health every time we earnestly pray and seek Him? Why don't we see everyone who seeks God being healed?

To answer these questions, I once more quoted Kuyper: "In that very fact, however sad, that so many cannot be cured, lies the medicine against unbelief. A very bitter medicine, that early or late grows on the grave of every one of us."[5]

I believe my motivating factor for asking these two additional questions was the fact that I couldn't understand how God had done so much for me when I was a baby, just to leave me with as many challenges as He had. In fact, wrestling with that was my motivating factor for selecting the topic for my paper in the first place. I was looking for an answer. I didn't find a comforting intellectual answer by using those historical theology works as my guide, so I concluded that each of us is just one more body and soul out of the billions of people God created, and since He makes us and can do whatever He wants with us, we can't assume that we can expect to be healed if we pray.

The odd thing about my coming to such a strong conclusion is that apparently, deep down I didn't really believe God was that uncaring. One incident that occurred at the time brought up an emotional response in me that conflicted with my intellectual conclusion. Just as

---
3. Ibid., 6.
4. Ibid., 5.
5. Ibid., 32.

I was nearing the end of my research for the paper, I discovered that a local organization was hosting a lecture on the topic of God and healing. I attended the lecture, and the main thing I recall was the speaker reading from 2 Chronicles 16:12 (NIV) concerning King Asa that "even in his illness he did not seek help from the Lord, but only from the physicians." The speaker's tone of voice changed toward the end of the quote. My perception was that he spoke the phrase "only from the physicians" with a cynical tone. A few people seated around me snickered. Instantaneously, what I would now call a righteous anger flared up in me, and I thought, *Is the implication that we should go to God and not just to a doctor when we have a need for healing so amusing?* Deep down, I still knew God cared and had done great things for me. Yet my struggle remained over why I had been left with the physical challenges I faced.

At this point in my writing process, I stopped into the professor's office, as he had requested, to let him know how I was progressing. He said to me, "Why don't you let me see what you've come up with?"

I gave him a typewritten draft with lots of handwritten corrections. The next time I stopped in his office, he handed me my draft with an A for effort on the top. He had written on the draft, "Good effort, these are complex questions that do confuse if not trouble most of us. I am not sure you fully answer the four questions you posed (vs. just asserting God's providence/sovereignty . . . which is an 'answer' to everything?) Still, this is a courageous, energetic, and thoughtful effort on matters that confuse if not trouble most of us. I hope you keep working on this . . . or does this answer all the questions you have?"

At the time, it didn't seem to me as if there were anything more to work on. In reality, the way I had approached researching and writing the paper just further cemented my view of God as the uncaring bus driver, despite the conflicting emotion that had risen up in me at the lecture. I was drifting farther away from my childlike wonderment at God and at the miracles of Jesus that I had felt when I was four years old. I also grew uneasy with pursuing becoming a pastor. I'm not sure exactly why. It just didn't seem like the right thing to do, so I didn't sign up for any additional courses.

In retrospect, not becoming a pastor at that point was one of the best decisions I ever made. In the coming decades, I was to have experiences that would bring me back to my childlike awe of what God has done, and Scriptures describing God as a loving Father would start jumping off the pages of the Bible at me. If I had become a pastor when I was young and had started preaching the personal theology I held at the time I wrote the paper, I would have deeply regretted it in the future.

In the Family Way

Beth and I decided at this point to stay with our current careers and move forward. Part of moving forward for us was our decision that it was time to start a family. With my history of having radiation, we had concerns about my ability to have children. If we did have children, would they be affected by the radiation? I brought this up to Dr. Brink, who was my doctor at the time. With my situation being an unusual case, he didn't have any medical textbooks that gave a clear answer. He told me he would send a letter of inquiry to a medical journal, with hopes that it would be answered.

When no answers were forthcoming, Beth and I decided once again not to live in fear and to go ahead and start our family. Without realizing it at the time (but as time would eventually tell), by deciding not to live in fear and to move ahead with life Beth and I had decided to create a family that would have to live by faith in the face of the unknown, just as our ancestors had.

About a year later, Beth began to suspect she was pregnant. I went with her to her appointment with the obstetrician, who happened to be the same doctor who had delivered me. We had been hiking, and Beth wore her hiking boots and a flannel shirt to the appointment. She was crying when she came back into the waiting room after seeing the doctor. I asked her what was wrong, and she said, "I'm so happy!"

Beth's pregnancy went well. The obstetrician knew my medical history. Besides delivering me he had also been my mother's doctor for years, so he had kept up on my status. He didn't feel it was necessary to request any tests or studies beyond what was usually done in that era.

Our daughter Anna was born on August 11, 1986. She was a healthy, normal child. Several months after Anna was born, I received a letter with an enclosure from Dr. Brink. It read, "I submitted your inquiry to the journal. They published the question and an answer in the Questions-and-Answers section. I copied this with the intention of sending it to you, and it simply submerged in a pile of papers on my desk."

The response in the journal stated, "The National Wilms' Tumor Study is currently assessing long-term effects of treatment of Wilms' tumor . . . However, since most children are under 6 years of age at the time of the diagnosis, it will take 20 to 30 years of follow-up to obtain complete data . . . At the present time, any effects on future offspring of Wilms' tumor survivors are speculative, since there are no data showing any increased abnormalities."[6]

After Anna was born, Beth changed her work hours from full time to being in the nursing resource pool. She worked two shifts a month so she could be a stay-at-home mom until the kids were in school. The two shifts a month held her job and kept her nursing skills up.

Beth had always been very healthy. Soon after Anna's birth, however, she began to get migraine headaches from time to time. Her doctor prescribed a medication that she could inject herself with when a migraine came on. A year after Anna was born, we found out Beth was pregnant again. Once again, her pregnancy was treated as a normal pregnancy and progressed well.

Our daughter Jan was born on March 31, 1988. She also was a healthy baby. In fact, when she was lying on her stomach in the hospital bassinet a couple of hours after she was born, she did a push-up and turned her head from one side to the other on the pillow!

---

6. *Journal of the American Medical Association* 255, no. 19 (May 1986): 2668.

At the time, we were attending the church I had grown up in. After Jan was born, we decided to join a congregation of the same denomination closer to our home, in the community of Cutlerville. I had grown up just a few miles away, but we were planning on sending the kids to a Christian school near our house and we thought it best that they went to church with kids who would be attending the same school.

In the middle of 1989, we found out Beth was pregnant with our third child. She was given a due date of mid-March. The pregnancy was going well until one night in the middle of January, when Beth woke me up. I heard her say, "I think my water broke."

I said, "The waterbed probably sprung a leak." It turned out the waterbed was fine. Beth was right. We made a phone call and headed for the hospital.

As we headed out the door, Beth picked up the teddy bear we had purchased for the baby. On the way to the hospital, she said, "This is way too early. This child doesn't even have a name."

At the hospital we were told women usually go into labor soon after their water breaks, but if labor does not start, infection usually sets in within forty-eight hours. This pregnancy was not far enough along for them to induce labor, so Beth was admitted to the hospital. The plan was to monitor her for signs of infection and let the pregnancy progress as far as possible.

My mom took care of Anna and Jan for us. The days started to pass. I would go to work every day, and after work go to the hospital to see Beth. I would also stop by my parents' place to see the girls every couple of days. My mother would help them cut out hearts and color pictures for their mom. I would bring these to the hospital and pin them to the corkboard in Beth's room. As the days turned into weeks, I started pinning hearts and pictures on top of hearts and pictures. After two weeks Beth had not developed an infection, but the threat was there constantly.

We were learning a lot about premature babies during Beth's hospital stay. The hospital had a book available that described all the scary complications that could come up with a premature birth.

Ultrasounds showed that our baby was growing at an accelerated rate, a good thing in this case, and was doing okay so far. Beth's hospital room had previously been an isolation room. It was located on a short hallway off the main unit and had another small, unused room separating it from the hallway, so it was very private and quiet. On Super Bowl Sunday evening, I was in the room with Beth. The last thing we wanted to do was watch the game. We had picked out both a boy's and girl's name. I made a bag of microwave popcorn, and we were playing chess. I recall that evening as being one of the most peaceful times we ever have had in our marriage.

After three weeks, we were told that the one factor of concern for a birth at that point would be lung development. If the baby's lungs were developed, it would be prudent to induce labor soon due to the ever-present threat of an infection. The only way to determine how developed the baby's lungs were was to do an amniocentesis and study cells indicating the level of lung development. An amniocentesis was attempted, but it turned out the placenta was positioned in such a way that a good sample couldn't be obtained. The decision was made to have Beth continue on bed rest and keep monitoring her for signs of infection. More ultrasounds were taken and evaluated.

At four weeks before the baby's due date, the doctor decided to induce labor. Beth started contractions naturally, however, on the morning the induction was scheduled. The birth process went as expected, but when our son, Eric, was actually born, the umbilical cord was twice as long as normal and was wrapped around his neck. He was born on February 14, 1990. He weighed seven pounds, eight ounces. All of our concern over possibly having him rushed off to the neonatal unit didn't become a reality. He went into the regular nursery.

During the next few days a whole lot of student nurses did their training assessments on Eric. He had hair on his lower back and faint fingerprints, as expected with an early birth. It was not often that students had access to premature babies, as these little ones usually wound up in the neonatal unit. This one they could get their hands on!

11. FILTERED THEOLOGY AND STARTING A FAMILY

Although the final month of the pregnancy had been a challenge and Eric had been born early, he did fine and grew well. When he was little and was still learning to talk, he would ask Beth, "Did you have me on Ballentine's Day because you loved me so much?"

Beth would hug him and say, "I love you, Eric."

12

The Downward Spiral

After Eric was born, Beth experienced a flare-up of migraines. The frequency and duration were very unpredictable. The self-injection medication she had previously been given was no longer effective. At this point, the migraines were frequent enough that her primary care doctor prescribed medication to prevent further migraines from occurring. This medication was not completely successful. She was also prescribed a different medication to "abort" a headache when one occurred. This was administered at the doctor's office by injection, when needed. Fortunately, it wasn't needed very often at first. Beth once went for a year without a migraine. We could even go on camping trips with the kids and things would be fine.

When our daughter Anna was six, she developed a fascination with manatees. Beth did some research and found out there was a manatee at Sea World in Ohio. She said, "We can leave early in the morning, put the kids in the car still asleep, and drive until they wake up. Then we'll only have to drive a few more hours before we get there."

My reply was, "Okay, but then we'll need to get the kids back home and they'll probably be awake for the whole trip!"

Eric was very young at the time and we weren't able to travel long distances without making some stops. But after thinking about it, Beth responded, "I think we can make it back."

My response was, "In that case, we might as well drive the same distance farther from home." We made plans to extend our trip into a camping adventure in West Virginia.

Our family car was a small 1986 Nova hatchback. One Saturday, I purchased a Sears cartop carrier to mount on the car. I was just finishing putting it together when Beth pulled in from work. "Quick," I said to the kids, "let's hide from your mom!" Somehow all four of us fit into the cartop carrier. I made sure the top was slightly open so we could get some air. The kids giggled, and I got a knee in my rib cage. "Quiet," I told the kids, "she's coming in the door!"

We could hear the door closing, and then Beth said, "Where is everyone?" As she came down the stairs looking for us, the kids couldn't resist letting out a giggle. Beth heard them, noticed the carrier was slightly open, and popped up the top.

"Surprise!" the kids yelled.

"There you are!" exclaimed Beth as our excited kids crawled out of the top carrier. Beth was genuinely surprised that we could all fit into that small space!

We dug out the tent Beth and I used for the backpack trip when we encountered the bear, and we loaded up the car. The five of us spent over a week on the road. We went to Sea World and made a circle of West Virginia. We drove the twisty, two-lane roads, with the kids enjoying the side-to-side motion of the car as we went into the curves. Once we were in the middle of a hard left hairpin turn when a sign on the side of the road came up showing a hard turn to the right symbol. I thought, *But I'm turning left. They don't have the correct sign up!* But the road never straightened out and immediately went into a hard hairpin turn to the right. If I had been driving a sports car, I might have enjoyed being on that stretch of road as much as the kids did!

We went to the New River and saw the New River Gorge bridge. We took a drive down into the valley by the bridge, where we could see people swinging off a rope attached to an abandoned bridge. There we found a small basin of water collecting runoff from a small creek before it flowed into the river. The spot was hidden by trees and brush. We camped in the area for a couple of days and were able to play in this water several times. The kids thought we were the only people who knew about it and it was our secret.

Later on the trip, we camped at a spectacular campground at

Seneca Rocks, toured a cave, and took a ride on a steam train on the Cass Scenic Railroad. When we got back home, my dad said to me, "You'll never regret going on that trip with the kids."

The Migraines Intensify

A few months after that wonderful family trip, Beth's migraines became more threatening and unpredictable. Beth's doctor quit her practice, so Beth had to find another primary care doctor. This doctor's office would administer a different IV medication to knock out a migraine when one would occur.

The Thanksgiving after I turned forty, I asked to get up in front of church and publicly thank God for how he had preserved me for forty years. Since we had switched congregations to one near our home, the people there didn't know my story. I spoke of what God had done for me when I was born, and then with the cyst in my hip before Beth and I were married.

The desire to get up and relate my thankfulness to the church this way surprised me a bit. I realized that God was protecting me throughout my life, but at the same time, I still viewed Him as picking me as the one who would have extra challenges to deal with. I saw Beth's migraines as one of those challenges for both of us.

Not long after that Thanksgiving, the frequency of the migraines Beth was experiencing slowly started to increase. She was referred to another doctor who was a specialist. This doctor believed the symptoms were hormone related. The course of treatment prescribed had no effect on the migraines. Beth also went in for acupuncture, which didn't help.

The Welcome Mistake

In the midst of dealing with Beth's new physical challenge of unpredictable, debilitating headaches coming up from time to time, I was made a deacon at church. One of the functions of a deacon was to be aware of situations that came up in the lives of church members where there was the possibility of financial need. The church could help in such circumstances, so I kept an eye out for them. At one point, one of the older ladies at the church became a widow. I looked up her phone number in the church directory and dialed the number. My intention was to set up a visit with her so I could find out how she was doing.

When the lady I called answered the phone, I identified myself as a deacon from the church and asked if she would like a visit. She said she would like that very much. Afterward, I realized that I had called another older member of the church who had the same name as the new widow. This older lady was living in a nursing home, and we hadn't ever met. My thought was, *How embarrassing is this? It wouldn't be right to cancel the visit. At least all I asked on the phone was if she would like a visit.*

I drove to the nursing home, found the woman's room, and knocked on her door. After she invited me in, we chatted a bit about the goings-on at church. Then she asked me, "So what prompted you to call and ask if you could visit?"

I could tell she was an intelligent and perceptive woman. I said, "I actually called you by mistake, but after that I figured you could use a visit as much as anyone."

"I'm glad you came!" was her response. As we continued to interact, she shared what her life was like at the nursing home. She appeared to me to be doing well, but she noted that she was starting to have problems reading standard text and she had always been a reader. She was not up to participating in most of the planned activities for the residents.

As we chatted, she also shared that the nursing home had arranged with the local college to have students interview the residents. The students were to write a paper on the life experiences of the resident they interviewed. She commented that the young man assigned to interview her had been a delight to interact with in the several visits she had with him. She shared a few more things that were of concern to her and then looked away a bit, and with a far-away tone in her voice said, "I can't do for God what I used to do. I really don't know why He keeps me here."

My response was, "I can tell you why you are here."

She turned her head, looked directly at me with a surprised look, and asked, "You can?"

"Yes," I said. "It's so you can share with people like the young man from the college what God has done for you." When she heard that, she got a big smile on her face.

During the drive home after the visit, I thought about how I had surprised myself by making such a simple and definite, spontaneous statement about why God was keeping this lady alive. I kept wondering what had motivated me to do so. Perhaps there was something deeper going on in me than what I was aware of?

A Cycle of Suffering

My parents purchased a small condo in Florida. Dad told me, "I did all the math. It costs about the same to own a condo as to rent one, but if you kids use it, that will make up the difference."

Mom and Dad spent several weeks in Florida painting, putting in extra wood trim, buying furnishings, and putting up wallpaper. Beth was doing well enough that we flew down in the early spring, after Mom and Dad were back home. It was a bit strange going to the condo. It was 1,400 miles from home and we had never been to the area. We pulled up to the gated community in a rental car. The security guard asked who we were. They looked us up and said, "You're on the list."

We drove the long entrance road with manicured golf fairways and ponds on both sides. We located the condo, got out of the car, and unlocked the door. Inside, there were notes with familiar handwriting and instructions for turning on the hot water heater and the air conditioner. It was a very nice, peaceful place. We opened the blinds to the sliding glass door and looked out a lanai (a small, screened in room) toward the well-kept golf course. We knew my parents had been getting things in order, but we hadn't really realized how significant their efforts were. What came to mind was Jesus saying He was going to prepare a place for us. It made me think about the fact that we really don't know what that means. We will probably be surprised at just how personal and spectacular that place He is preparing really will be.

That week, Beth developed a nagging migraine. On Sunday, we attended a church service at the local community banquet center. An established Presbyterian church several miles away was holding these services with the intention of starting a new church in this growing location. Communion was served at the service. At one point the pastor said, "Come forward to partake of the elements. I will be off to the side with oil to anoint anyone seeking healing."

After taking Communion, we returned to our seats. Beth whispered to me, "I'm going up." We got up and went up to the pastor. He anointed her with oil, and we returned to our seats. Little changed, and in the next few days Beth's discomfort increased. The migraine dampened much of the trip. On the way home on the plane, Beth was curled up on the seat, with her eyes covered to keep the light from increasing her level of discomfort.

Eventually, the migraine pain Beth experienced turned into a cycle of eight days on and eight days off. If she was scheduled to work at any point during the eight days of pain, she managed to go in and complete her shift. Many of the days she wasn't scheduled to work she spent in bed.

Passing on a Gift

With Beth becoming debilitated periodically, we would have a few people from church offer to bring us a meal from time to time. We would tell them we were doing all right, but if they insisted, we would accept. One of the elderly widow ladies brought us a meal. I went out to her car to bring it in. She had placed the meal containers in a large paper grocery sack with a white envelope with our name on it taped to the side. She said, "Make sure you don't throw that envelope away."

We assumed that the envelope contained a card. After she left, we opened it up and it contained a check for $1,000! I said to Beth, "We're doing all right. How do we tell her we don't need the money, and how do we get her to take the check back?"

Beth and I discussed the situation after we ate the meal. A few weeks beforehand, one of the ladies at church had given birth to twins. Beth made the comment that if someone from church offered to buy a twin stroller for the family, should they turn it down just because they could afford to buy one? As I thought this over, it came to me that not wanting to accept the money was a matter of pride.

The next evening, Beth called the lady who had delivered the meal. The two of them arranged a time for us to bring her dishes back. When we dropped the dishes off, the lady invited us to stay and chat. After a few minutes of conversation, she asked, "Did you open the envelope?"

I answered, "Yes, we did. We will accept your gift on a few conditions. We're getting by financially. We want you to know that you may see us go to Florida this winter, if Beth is up to it. If that bothers you, we'd like to give the check back to you. The second thing we want you to know is that if you want us to keep the money and you ever need it, let us know and we'll give it back to you. The last thing is, we are planning on passing this money on to others in need, as we are financially able."

Her response was, "I can see my investment is paying off already."

Trying Everything without Success

One evening, Beth was dropping Eric off at a junior high skating party when she sensed some sort of force coming into the car and nausea quickly coming on (I'll talk more about that in the next chapter). The migraine pain came on with full force. After a few days, she called her primary care doctor to let her know what was happening. Beth said, "I know this will go away, it always does." But this time, it did not.

Beth continued taking the medications from her primary care provider. They did little to relieve the pain. While still under her doctor's care, and with her knowledge, Beth went to see another doctor who had graduated from medical school but was combining traditional medical training with alternative medicine. Experiencing so much pain and so little relief, she was seeking an answer outside what the mainstream medical community would normally provide. This new doctor Beth visited had several potential causes in mind for the migraines. One by one, treatments were prescribed for each cause. When the treatment for one cause proved ineffective, he would cross that potential cause off his list and try treating Beth for another potential cause. Most of what the doctor prescribed was indeed outside the mainstream and wasn't covered by insurance, and we were running up large bills. After several different treatments proved ineffective, Beth's nursing intuition told her it was time to turn to the medical mainstream once again.

Beth was then sent to a neurologist who prescribed steroids that worked for a few weeks. After these became ineffective, he injected Botox into Beth's forehead. The Botox was ineffective. He tried her on steroids again at a different dose, and this time the steroids were ineffective. The next thing he tried was a nerve block into the top of her head. Twenty injections were administered at one appointment. The doctor said he could tell who really was in pain by who was willing to endure the pain of the injections. After the nerve block also proved ineffective, he tried at least half a dozen powerful medications to knock out the pain. They varied in their effectiveness, and Beth's actual level of relief was minimal. Finally, this doctor said he had no other answers for her. We needed to look elsewhere.

Beth took a leave of absence from work in October 2004. Her pain made it difficult for her to get to sleep, and I would disturb her at night. Light sensitivity during the day also increased the pain. She hurt so much that she just wanted to be isolated and didn't care where she slept, as long as she could get to sleep. She started sleeping on a couch in a spare bedroom that had only one window to keep darkened. She spent much of each day on that couch as well. The couch met her needs, and its cushioned back provided her with a sense of comfort. She kept a cordless phone next to the couch, but I never even thought about putting a bed in the room. I didn't want us to come to the point where we viewed this arrangement as a permanent situation.

Beth's primary care physician referred her to a pain clinic in Grand Rapids. The doctor at the pain clinic stated that Beth was in a state of rebound in which her nerves would become hypersensitized by cycles of flare-ups and medication doses. Beth was taken off most of the medications she had previously been prescribed over the years. This would allow her nerve endings to come out of the state of rebound. As an RN, Beth understood that these types of medications were not able to correct a problem permanently and then no longer be needed. They were prescribed in an effort to improve quality of life at least short-term, and since they had not done so, she was eager to get off them. She was given other medications during that time to keep the pain down and reset her nervous system.

For six weeks during this process Beth was unable to be alone, so she lived with my parents for most of that time. They would bring her twice a day to the pain clinic to have the medications administered by IV. She had an IV catheter in her arm that would stay in from day to day. One of the medications she was given was steroids again. This really drove her appetite. When I went to see her one night, she had a huge bowl of pecan ice cream and she was licking her lips. She gained a significant amount of weight from being on the steroids.

On Thanksgiving Day that year, Beth's pain was especially severe. Any light would make it worse. I put a tarp up over the window in the room with the couch, to make it totally dark. We contacted the pain clinic doctor. He was traveling and called us from an airport. He gave us instructions for changing her levels of medication. This change did not have much of an effect. When Beth visited the pain clinic after Thanksgiving, the attendant at the patient pick-up struck up a conversation with her while she was waiting for my mother to drive up. He asked, "Did you have a good Thanksgiving?"

Beth said, "No."

He then asked, "Did you have any turkey?"

Beth said, "No."

He was feeling awkward and was looking for something positive, so he asked, "Did you have any dressing?"

Her response was, "No."

"Did you have any pie?"

Beth said, "No," and started to sob.

A cold compress seemed to help with the pain a bit. Bags of frozen peas could mold to the shape of Beth's forehead. From this, we switched to a machine that circulated cold water. My mom had used it after surgery on her shoulder. This was a small cooler that I would fill with ice and water. It had tubes connected to a sleeve that you could put over the affected area, and a pump to circulate the water. This would keep cold for a couple of hours. Taking care of Beth, I remember thinking, *This must be what it's like to have a wife in a nursing home.*

After Beth was out of rebound, she was prescribed several new medications to prevent the migraines. In reality, that meant the meds were supposed to reduce the level of pain, because it never went away. In addition to the preventative medication, another "new" medication was prescribed to deal with the pain when it peaked.

The pain clinic program also required Beth to meet with a psychologist. The psychologist counseled Beth to visualize places she had a happy memory of, to take her mind off the pain. Beth found this very difficult to do, and that approach didn't work for her. The psychologist next wanted to hypnotize her. Beth refused because she didn't want to be in an altered state of mind, even temporarily.

The Christmas Blizzard

After attempting to fine-tune a medication program for Beth for several months without success, the pain clinic doctor arranged a consultation with a nationally recognized pain institute several hours away from home. We made the trip for an initial consultation, and afterward her medications were rearranged again. The institute also prescribed physical therapy, which Beth arranged to do back home.

At one point a couple of months later, Beth's pain went away just before we traveled to a follow-up appointment at the consulting pain institute. It was Christmas break, and we decided to keep going after the appointment and drive the family to Florida since Beth was doing well. There was a blizzard the day before our appointment. The worst of the snowstorm was south of us, but the roads to the clinic had been cleared. As we sat in the clinic's waiting room, we watched news reports on television showing trucks blocking the interstate heading south. We were hearing nothing about any issues on a parallel interstate about 150 miles away, so that road became our new route of choice.

In the appointment, the doctors were pleased that Beth was doing well. But they also believed this reprieve from pain was temporary. Beth stayed on the recommended treatment plan, and the doctors took a wait-and-see attitude.

When we left the clinic, we drove to our selected parallel route and headed south on the interstate. When we crossed the state line it was getting dark, the temperature was plummeting, and the interstate turned into a snowy two-track. We were driving through the country and saw no one on the road. About 7:00 p.m. we spotted a gas station sign lighting up the night. We pulled off. The cashier looked up in surprise that someone had come in. He said the crossroad had not been plowed beyond the highway overpass. We paid for the gas, along with a gallon of window washer fluid, and got back on the road. We stopped at a deserted rest area, and in the lobby a loudspeaker was repeating warnings about hazardous driving conditions.

Hearing that, we decided it was time to find a motel. We drove for miles with no motel in sight. It was December 23, and one of the kids suggested that we could sleep in a barn the way Mary and Joseph had. My reply was, "We might wish we had a barn to sleep in."

We came to spot where the road was extremely icy. There were temporary *ROAD CLOSED* barricades on the highway. A state trooper was directing traffic up the off ramp. That interchange had several motels. We went from one to another, and each one was full. There was a Good Samaritan person in a Jeep who saw us driving slowly and flagged us down. He told us all the motels were full. Our only option was to go back ten miles to the nearest interchange that would have other motels. It took us close to an hour to make the journey.

The first motel we checked was full. So was the second. But the clerk at the second motel told us of a business motel that didn't advertise on the highway. He speculated that it might have rooms available, but he didn't have the phone number. We pulled into the business motel parking lot around 10:30 p.m. There were three people in line at the desk in front of us. I heard the manager tell the attendant not to give out certain rooms because one of the housekeeping people had not made it in and rooms couldn't be given to people without being cleaned. He was not sure how many rooms were left.

As the desk attendant was checking people in, the phone kept ringing with people inquiring about rooms. More people had come in the door behind us too. When the third call came in, I stepped past a woman holding a baby in front of me and addressed the attendant. "You have a lot of people who are here right now," I said. "Shouldn't you make sure they have rooms before you take phone reservations?"

The attendant looked at me and then said into the phone, "You'll have to call back."

The woman with the baby turned to me and said, "Thank you!"

We managed to get a room, and as we went to the elevator to find our room the lobby was starting to resemble a disaster response center. People were sitting on the floor and falling asleep on blankets they had brought in from their cars.

The next morning was a bright, cold day. The thermometer stood at 6 degrees. We were told the interstate was closed, but the state highway was open. We had to drive east to connect with the state highway. Once on the highway we made progress, until after ten miles we came to a crossroad. Beyond the intersection a truck had slid into the ditch and was blocking the road. This happened to be right next to the interchange on the interstate where we were turned back the night before. I thought, *Well, we can get on the interstate and go back to the same motel. The kids can swim in their pool.*

Then I noticed cars going down the southbound on-ramp. We followed them at 45 miles an hour for about 3 miles. After that, the road was ice. It looked as if someone had taken ice-cream scoops, frozen water in them, and put the ice on the road. There were two other vehicles traveling this road. We were moving between 5 and 10 miles an hour and stayed about 150 yards apart. We had only a couple of water bottles to drink from. These were the ones in the cooler. The cooler insulated them from freezing, unlike the ones outside the cooler. From time to time we would have to stop and wait for a National Guard wrecker to pull out a semi. I was glad we had filled the gas tank late the night before. One time when we were stopped a helicopter came near, hovered awhile, and left.

By midafternoon, we made it far enough south that the temperature was up past freezing. The next issue to deal with was going through southern Tennessee and having massive chunks of ice falling from trees onto the highway from time to time. Fortunately, none hit our van. We found a motel room in southern Georgia for the night.

When we woke up, it was Christmas morning. In the continental breakfast room of the motel the TV was set to CNN. We were making our self-serve waffles when the caption "Stranded Motorist on I-65" came on the screen. Above the caption was a van looking strangely like ours, surrounded by nothing but white. It appeared that this was our one moment of fame on national TV, and no one knew it but us. Perhaps that's a good thing.

Beth's parents were wintering in Florida. They were excited when we were able to surprise them with a visit on Christmas! Beth did well with the stress of the trip. She did well the entire trip, until we came to Chattanooga on the way back. Then the pain set in again.

At home, the doctor at the pain clinic in Grand Rapids conferenced with the doctors at the pain institute where we had traveled for the consultation. The decision was made for the pain clinic to turn Beth's course of treatment over to the institute. Beth was prescribed more drugs. One of these could react with overripe fruit and cause a reaction that could be fatal. We had to purchase a medical alert bracelet for her. I stared at it and wondered if we were stuck with this situation for the rest of our lives.

Beth was given one drug she could only take two times a week since greater frequency would risk her becoming dependent on it. On the days she took this drug, she was able to get off the couch and do some household tasks. Once a month, we were scheduled to make the long drive to the pain institute. I would purposely not remember the exit number off the highway from one trip to the next. This would frustrate Beth. It was my way of refusing to give in to the fact that this was beginning to look like a hopeless, permanent situation.

At the pain institute appointments, Beth would see the pain doctor and have a session with a psychologist. A visit to the clinic was a full day's trip. At one visit, the doctor and psychologist appointments were several hours apart. It was a rainy day, so to fill the time we drove to a park and lay in the back of our van. We held each other and listened to the rain, wondering if Beth's pain would ever be gone and if we would ever have a normal life.

Tight Money and Intolerable Pain

With the reduction of income from Beth being on disability, I really felt money was tight. We were also paying for parochial high school for three kids, and college bills coming up in the fall. Even twenty dollars for gas to get to the institute seemed big at the time. One morning when we were scheduled to travel to the pain institute, I went to the gas station just as soon as it opened. As I was filling my tank, a lady approached me and asked if I could give her some gas money.

I looked in my billfold. I had two twenties and three ones. I offered her the three ones.

She asked me if I could give her more because she had to drive farther than three dollars' worth of gas would take her.

I went into the station and asked the attendant to make change for a twenty. The attendant said that they hadn't been to the bank and couldn't make change. I thought, *Who ever heard of a gas station not being able to break a twenty?*

I went back out to the gas pumps. The lady appeared to have a legitimate need. I didn't have the heart to tell her three dollars was all I would give her. I handed her a twenty and found myself saying, "Here, take a twenty. Jesus loves you."

As I got into my car I thought, *Where did that come from?* If asked, I would have said I still viewed God as the dysfunctional school bus driver. For some reason, when I gave this lady an amount of money that really meant something to me, how important it was for her to know that Jesus loved her just came out of my mouth.

There were two times Beth's pain flared up high enough that we went to the local emergency room. In the ER, she would be given some medications and released. The main effect of these medications was to make her go to sleep, with the hope that the pain would be at a tolerable level when she woke up

The pain institute didn't like what the local ER administered and didn't want Beth to make repeat visits there. If the institute couldn't reduce the number of days a month that a patient had tolerable pain, they had an inpatient program where they would take patients off all the medication they were on. The doctors would then administer a single medication at a high dosage rate and note the effect. They would then taper it down and do the same with another drug in an attempt to determine the best combination of drugs. We knew a woman who had gone through this process. She said it nearly killed her. All the same, Beth was told to bring along enough clothes for an extended stay when she came to her next appointment at the institute.

At the next visit, Beth presented the record of her pain levels to the doctor. She had suffered quite a few very bad days the previous month. At the end of the visit, the doctor had his hand on the knob of the exam room door and said, "I'll have the nurse came back and set up your next appointment."

I asked him, "Why aren't you talking about Beth being admitted?"

He looked at Beth and told her, "The inpatient process doesn't usually result in a pain rate any better than what you had last month. Let's monitor how you do."

We were thankful for that news. Beth had dreaded the thought of going through the traumatic experience of the inpatient ordeal alone, several hours from home. Still, every day without a solution for her was an ordeal in itself.

13

Spiritual Showdowns, Heavenly Healings

In the fall of 2004, I was dealing with helping our daughter Anna select a college and figuring out how to pay for it. The college she was most interested in was Trinity Christian College in Palos Heights, Illinois. Beth really wanted to be part of life, so one day when the college was holding an informational meeting in our area, she put on her dark glasses and we went to the meeting even though she was in severe pain. As we were driving to the meeting I couldn't help thinking, *With three kids in parochial school this year and Beth not working, we are barely making it. If Anna goes to this college, our total bill for all the kids will be at least twice as high next year.*

The college was a good fit for Anna. She wanted to become a Spanish teacher, and the school had an excellent program for it. Anna had taken Advanced Placement (AP) classes and advanced Spanish courses. If Anna chose Trinity, the college would award credit for these directly toward her major. This would enable her to obtain multiple teaching credentials in the standard four-year college time frame.

One thing they mentioned at the meeting that caught my attention was the fact that students with high grades and ACT scores were invited to apply for a Founders Scholarship, which would completely pay for tuition. This scholarship was awarded based on a committee reviewing each applicant's academic record, along with a paper the student wrote, and the student's history of charitable service. Two of these scholarships were to be awarded, and only about twenty students were eligible to apply for the award. Anna happened to be one of them. Even though God seemed far away to me at the time, I thought, *This must be the way God plans on providing for us, by having Anna win the scholarship.*

A few months later we went to another meeting where the names of the scholarship winners were announced. I felt really let down when Anna was not one of the two students who received the Founders Scholarship. She was awarded a Presidential Scholarship, which would pay a little more than a third of the total cost of tuition and room and board. *I guess we will make it through somehow*, I thought.

The Craziest Phone Call

By then, I was a counselor in our church boys' club. The club would hold a Pinewood Derby for the boys, including a separate race for just the adult leaders who wanted to build a car. Throughout the winter, I worked on my derby car from time to time. I put a lot of work into that car. It became more than just a pastime. Working on my car became a way to get my mind off Beth's situation for a while. With everything in life looking hopeless, I really wanted to have something positive happen like winning the race.

In the spring, I received a phone call from another person involved in the boys' club. The caller said I was going to think this was the craziest phone call I had ever received. He told me he was concerned about Beth's condition. He said he was related to a woman who also had struggled with chronic migraines, and nothing had helped her either. He told me his family had found a pastor who had the gift of discerning of spirits and also gifts of healings (see 1 Corinthians 12:1–11). This pastor had been praying with this other woman, and she was doing a lot better. The pastor was from out of state, but he was coming into town for a couple of weeks to pray with people.

Beth and I discussed this and concluded that anyone who was a sincere Christian and wanted to pray with us was welcome to do so.

This caller's father was hosting a meeting with the visiting pastor in his home. I called his father up and asked if we could attend.

"Sure, we have room for you," he replied. "If we have more than ten or fifteen people show up, we'll use our basement."

The prayer meeting was the next Sunday evening. The Saturday beforehand was the annual area-wide running of the Pinewood Derby. This event also included an extra race set up for adults from all the clubs in the area so they could compete against each other. Just as when I was young and was winning the derby race that had meant so much to me, round after round the derby car I had worked on so hard kept winning. The final round came, and my car crossed the finish line almost half a car length ahead of the next fastest car. I was awarded the first-place trophy. After the event, I carried my derby car and trophy back to my car and thought, *Is this all I have in my life is a piece of wood?*

Sunday evening, Beth was in considerable pain when I helped her into our car to leave for the prayer meeting. When we arrived we found cars lined up on both sides of the street in front of the home where the meeting was being held. After walking about fifty yards from where we had parked, we arrived at the house and found the basement packed with people. As we were waiting for the meeting to start, I was observing the guest pastor. He looked like a cross between Colonel Sanders and Santa Claus. He was chatting with someone about signs of the end times. I was beginning to wonder how legitimate this meeting was going to be.

The guest pastor was introduced. He was Bill Putnam from North Dakota. Pastor Bill, as he liked to be called, started the meeting with a teaching time. The text he referenced was Daniel 10, with an emphasis on verses 12–15. This passage speaks of Daniel humbling himself and praying for understanding. An angel speaking to Daniel says that since the first day that Daniel had set his mind to gain understanding, his words had been heard. But when this angel was coming to Daniel in response, the prince of the Persian kingdom had resisted him for twenty-one days, until the archangel Michael came to help him break through to Daniel.

Pastor Bill explained that Satan is the prince of this world, and that the prince of the Persian kingdom represented the evil spiritual forces at work in Persia. He also explained Nebuchadnezzar's dream of the image with the head of gold, chest of silver, belly and thighs of bronze, legs of iron, and feet of iron and clay. He pointed out the spiritual forces of evil at work in the historical empires described in Daniel's vision. His point was, "For we do not wrestle against flesh and blood, but against principalities, against powers, against the rulers of the darkness of this age, against spiritual hosts of wickedness in the heavenly places" (Ephesians 6:12 NKJV).

As he moved into the healing prayer time, Pastor Bill said that we cannot manipulate God. He stated that when we ask the Holy Spirit to be involved in a healing, it is usually speeded up. Something that normally would take six months to heal might take two. Something that normally would take a month might take a week or two, or even a few days. Then he added, "If something happens tonight, it's a miracle!"

When it was our time to go forward, Pastor Bill asked Beth, "What do you need prayer for?" We sat in two chairs in front of him, and she explained her situation. The host of the meeting anointed her with oil, and Pastor Bill prayed for her. As soon as she was anointed, Beth's pain level shot up even higher, and she held her head in her hands for a few moments.

After praying for Beth, Pastor Bill asked me, "What's your prayer need?" I answered that I needed grace to deal with Beth's situation. I also said that due to surgery and radiation for kidney cancer as a newborn (the Wilms tumor), I had heavy scar tissue, a tilted pelvis, one leg longer than the other, and a spinal curvature. Because I was forty-four years old, I added, all my bone lengths were fixed, so I realized that probably nothing could be done.

Pastor Bill looked right at me and said, "The Holy Spirit can do a lot for you." He called everyone to gather around and watch. He anointed me and said, "Put out your arms." He had me put out my arms and lightly hold my palms together. Then he lightly touched the back of my hands and commanded my shoulders to align, in Jesus' name. I felt a little something but didn't think too much of it.

"Pick up your feet," Pastor Bill then said. He took my heels in the palms of his upturned hands and said, "I push up a little; I don't pull. In a few seconds, I'm going to command your scar tissue to soften and your left hip to drop an inch, in Jesus' name." As he commanded the spirit of asymmetry to come out of my body, my left foot started to move downward until both feet were even. Everyone who had gathered around could see it happen.

As soon as I stood up, I felt as if an electric shock had gone through me from about six inches above the knees to the bottom of my feet. I was also wobbling around with my arms out, trying to keep my balance. "Wow," I said, "this is really different!"

Pastor Bill had two more people seated in front of him by then, but he smiled at me and said, "Sometimes it takes a while to sink in."

We had been told this was a "come and go as you need to" meeting, and not knowing what to think or do next, Beth and I left. As we walked across the front lawn, in her mind Beth was wondering why she was in worse pain than before and I was trying to catch my balance. On the drive home, I kept missing my shifts in my stick shift car. The feel of the clutch releasing had changed after my hip had come down. My left foot was an inch closer to the clutch pedal than normal.

No Lift Needed!

The following week was quite a week. Monday morning when I was getting ready to go to work, I took my left work shoe and pulled out the lift inside. Many years earlier, my right knee had begun to give me problems. I was told that due to the way my skeletal structure ended up, instead of a normal stride I was jamming my right leg every time I took a step. The doctor had decided that a lift in the left shoe would even out the bottoms of my shoes. He knew this would also have the adverse side effect of increasing the stress on my spine and muscles. However, he thought the benefit for my knee long-term would be greater than the adverse effect on my spine. He left the final decision on this up to me. I thought it would be worth trying. When the lift was first put in my shoe, it felt as if a two-by-four piece of lumber had been strapped to the bottom of my shoe, and I could feel my spine shift. But after a few weeks, I became used to the lift and it seemed to become a permanent part of who I was.

Now, I pulled the lift out of my shoe and stared at it. I had been living a relatively normal life and had not gone to the healing service to seek healing for myself, but rather for Beth. I was getting along okay, but now I had a decision to make. I had to either trust what had happened to me or leave the lift in the shoe. I tossed the lift on the table, put on my shoe, and went to work. I found that with my pelvis in a lower position on my left side when I walked, I could feel some muscles that needed to be developed a bit. I would have to think about actively rolling my weight to the ball of my left foot. After a few days my muscles started adjusting to my "new normal," and walking without the shoe lift felt natural. I never once put the lift back in my shoe.

That week, I stopped in our pastor's office. I explained what had happened to me and said, "Help me understand this. If Jesus is the only mediator between God and man, and we are not supposed to seek spiritists or mediums, why did this take place as it did?" (See Leviticus 19:31.)

Our pastor replied, "You said that the visiting pastor didn't claim to be able to manipulate God. This is different than what the Bible describes as the spiritists and mediums we're not supposed to have anything to do with." He then said, "Would you have recognized this healing as coming from the hand of God if it just came on slowly?"

Reflecting on his question, I realized that I would not have. The same week, in a rare visit to the kitchen (because she wasn't usually well enough to be involved in there), Beth noticed the lift from my shoe on the kitchen table. She asked me why I wasn't wearing it. I told her it was because my toes were the same distance from my nose. She looked at my back and could tell that the curve in my lower back was gone. She hadn't realized that a physical change had taken place after the meeting. Over the years, five doctors had said nothing could be done for my condition. Now, I was relearning to drive my stick shift car because my left foot was putting the clutch in faster than I was used to. I was also waking myself up in the night when my ankle bones would bang together in my sleep. Before my healing, my bones were not lined up and this didn't happen. After a few days, my body adjusted to it.

In the middle of the week, the host of the healing service called. "How is your wife doing?" he asked.

"Actually," I replied, "she's not doing very well."

The caller's response was, "At times, God grants these types of healings in stages, to help us understand that we're to keep seeking Him." Then he asked, "How are you doing?"

I said that for Beth and me, seeing the changes in my legs seemed like God's way of showing us that He still had His hand on our lives. I told him I could really feel and see the changes, but that my shoulders were still not square with the rest of my body.

"God is a God of completeness," the host said in response to that. "I encourage you both to come back on Saturday for another meeting!"

Getting to the Bottom of Things

Saturday came and we were unable to go the teaching time of the meeting, but we arrived at the start of the healing time. The basement was packed once again. When it was our turn to come forward, Beth mentioned some things to Pastor Bill that she had been wrestling with for nearly as long as she could remember.

"Now we're getting to the bottom of it," he told her. He stated that she was under the influence of a specific evil spirit that had been affecting her ancestors for three generations (see Exodus 20:5). Based on the type of spirit he described and her family history, Beth could see that this was true. She was anointed once again. This time, she did not experience the increase in pain when she was anointed. Pastor Bill commanded this spirit to leave her, in Jesus' name. As the influence of this spirit left her, she felt as if a dam had suddenly broken inside her. She experienced a period of weeping during which she had no control. Later, she realized that this spirit had begun to affect her early in life.

Pastor Bill then asked me if I wanted prayer for anything. I commented that he had spent a lot of time with Beth and there were many others waiting. The host whispered to me, "Go ahead and ask," so I mentioned my shoulders.

Pastor Bill then said, "Sit back in your chair again and stretch out your arms." He again anointed me and touched the back of my hands, as he had done before. He once again commanded my shoulder bones to move, in Jesus' name.

We had been told that Pastor Bill had the gift of having the Holy Spirit reveal what was happening as it happened. This time, he commented on the movement as the Holy Spirit moved my bones back and forth to bring them into alignment. First about my left shoulder, he said, "It's moving forward; now it's moving back." Then about my right shoulder, he said, "It's moving forward; now it's moving back." He spoke in a tone as though this degree of movement was all he expected.

I could feel my shoulder blade continue to move. Pastor Bill continued, "Now it's moving way back; now it's moving even farther!" When it was all the way back, it felt as if someone had put a pipe wrench on my shoulder blade and twisted it. It was a distinct and powerful, but not painful sensation that I will never forget.

Before we left, Pastor Bill spent some time advising the two of us about how to deal with our situation. He spoke of how God sees us as cleansed in Christ, and that we are to use the weapons of spiritual warfare to deal with the doubts and challenges that the forces of spiritual evil throw at us. He spoke of how Satan is the master of lies and will seek to deceive us. He told me, "Whenever the devil comes around to torment your wife, you have the authority to tell him to leave." I thought, *Who am I to do that?*

The next weeks were a struggle as we continued to marvel at what had happened to me, yet Beth continued to struggle with pain that ranged from moderate to severe. I recall one night at the boys' club meeting when I was talking with another leader. I was sitting on a table and picked up my feet to show him that my feet were even. "I don't get it," I said. "I took Beth to a healing service for her. I get a miracle, and she's in the same situation."

He shook his head and said, "Go figure."

One of the requirements of my job was to work a twelve-hour night shift once a month on a Saturday night. I was driving to work one Saturday evening to fulfill my obligation. In a rare moment of not having Beth's situation in the front of my mind, I was thinking about how to stay awake until morning. Halfway to work I heard, *Am I not the same God who watched over you when you were little?*

My response was, *That was different.*

I received a one-word response: *How?*

I had no answer.

The Healing Rooms

One day, I called the man who hosted the healing services. At the end of the conversation, he mentioned that he had just gotten home from the "Healing Rooms." I asked him what the Healing Rooms were. He explained that this was the name for an organization of volunteers who got together and prayed for people, to help them deal with the same type of issues as Pastor Bill prayed for. He also reminded me that healing is a process, while miracles are immediate.

The Saturday after this phone call, Beth was in severe pain. I loaded her up and took her to the Healing Rooms. Here, after being assigned to a person, two or three volunteers would pray together on their own first, and then as a team they would meet the person who had come in and they would minister to him or her privately.

The lead volunteer who met with us gave us about forty-five minutes of personalized teaching time. He said that most Christians don't realize that Jesus has already accomplished our physical healing on the cross, just as He accomplished our salvation. Just as we seek spiritual healing in this life, we can seek the manifestation of physical healing in this life too, knowing we will have full healing in the next life. He referenced the Scripture text telling us to ask, seek, and knock (found in Luke 11:1–13). He also taught us to be careful how we word our prayers. He said not to pray, *God, You could heal me if You wanted* to, but to pray, *God, I know You are my Healer. I know You will heal me in Your time*—realizing His time might be the next life.

This seems like a very minor point, but when people have a long-term illness or condition, after a while they can start to think that God must not even love them—because they know He has the power to heal, but they don't see it happen. This change in how we pray keeps us in the proper perspective. God will heal, but He has His timing for His purposes.

The Healing Rooms volunteer also presented Beth with several Scripture texts that spoke of how much God loves her. Beth said that those texts certainly didn't seem to apply to her. As Pastor Bill had done, this volunteer spoke of the lies Satan would have us believe. In this case, Beth was believing that God's promises didn't apply to her. He then said he was going to command a deaf-and-dumb spirit to leave her because she could hear and she could talk, but when she read these promises in the Bible, they weren't revealed to her in her spirit.

The volunteer anointed Beth and commanded this deaf-and-dumb spirit to leave her, in Jesus' name. At the close of this visit, he said that she needed to be bathed in prayer and reminded daily of the promises God gives us in His Word. He gave Beth a five-page handout with these Scripture promises on them and told her to read them out loud three times a day. He taught us that the devil doesn't know what we *think* in our heads. Yet when we read the Bible *out loud* and pray *out loud*, the devil is able to hear us and knows we are calling upon the name of Jesus. He invited us to return to the Healing Rooms as many times as needed.

Beth read the passages of Scripture, as she had been instructed. I still viewed putting a bed for her in the spare bedroom as admitting that her condition would be permanent, so she was still living on the couch in the dark room. She would tuck the Scripture handout from the Healing Rooms under the couch, along with a small flashlight. Three times a day she would feel under the couch, find the document and the flashlight, and speak aloud God's Word recorded on the handout.

Early the next week, Beth was reading the handout and suddenly exclaimed, "This applies to me!"

"Yeah," I said, "it does," wondering why she couldn't see it before.

Dealing with Return Symptoms

About this time, something interesting happened. One of the teachings on the handout was that we can be healed and that afterward, the devil will try to give us the same symptoms as before to make us think we haven't been healed. Honestly, this didn't make sense to us. If people have the symptoms, they have the problem, right?

We were to learn differently firsthand. My scar tissue started to contract, and over several days great tension was developing between my rib cage and my pelvis, much the way it had felt prior to my healing. One morning, I was asking myself if I had ever actually prayed for this specific condition. I realized I had not. I started to pray for this, and before I said *Amen* the extra tension was gone.

Beth continued to struggle with head pain. About two weeks after our first visit to the Healing Rooms, we returned. The volunteer who met with us on this visit said that after a spirit is cast out it will try to return, as Jesus described in Matthew 12:43–45. He told us, "You need to rebuke the devil when he comes to torment you."

I stated what I had been thinking after our second meeting with Pastor Bill: "Who are we to rebuke the devil?"

To answer my question, the volunteer then taught us more about the spirit world we contend with in spiritual warfare. He referenced Matthew 4:1–11, where Jesus quoted Scripture and rebuked the devil. He read from Luke 9 and 10 and pointed out that the Twelve and the Seventy were given the authority to cast out demons and did so. He also noted that apparently, they had not yet even been taught the proper way to pray, because Jesus teaching them the Lord's Prayer is recorded later in Luke.

The volunteer was pointing out that this type of authority is given to believers. Rebuking must be done in the name of the Lord Jesus Christ whenever Satan comes around. He taught us that this didn't apply only to this situation with our health, but to any situation where there is a roadblock to having the proper relationship with Jesus.

Facing the Tormentor

After this visit, Beth truly began to believe that the only way she was going to find relief from the pain was to rebuke Satan and completely humble herself and pray for the Holy Spirit to heal her. It was at this time that we began to rebuke Satan to break the pain. The first time we did this, we took our van to the parking lot of a local park for a quiet location. We prayed, telling God that despite the instruction we had received, we really didn't think we were prepared to rebuke Satan—so God would have to give us the words.

After that prayer, I started to rebuke the devil. It was an intense time where Beth and I both were directly facing our tormentor. I told Satan to "leave my wife alone" and to "flee from her, in Jesus' name." After this, Beth's pain subsided significantly for a short period of time. It flared up again, and I rebuked the devil once more. Again, the pain faded for a while.

This type of praying and rebuking went on for several days. At the time, we honestly didn't know if the changes in Beth's pain were a natural thing or were caused by the rebuking. If the rebuking was the cause, why did the pain come back? Then we remembered Pastor Bill's words: "Rebuke the devil *whenever* he comes around."

At this point, we realized that we were engaged in active spiritual warfare. Beth also realized that when things happened like the force coming into the car a couple of years earlier and her migraine pain locking in as a result, what she had been dealing with was a spiritual force. She now knew that it was a demonic force. Beth started engaging in spiritual warfare on her own, even when I was at work. She would read Scripture aloud and tell Satan to flee from her, in Jesus' name. The verse she quoted was James 4:7 (NIV), "Resist the devil, and he will flee from you." She told Satan she had the power and authority in the name of Jesus to command him and his demons to flee.

While Beth was at the Healing Rooms, she examined and

understood the lies that Satan had led her to believe since she was a young girl. She would tell Satan that he is the master of lies, he is the one who steals kills and destroys, and he is a stumbling block and doesn't have in mind the things of God, but the things of men (see John 8:44; John 10:10; Matthew 16:23). Then she would declare that Jesus is greater than he is (see 1 John 4:4), and that she believed God's Word rather than Satan's lies.

After rebuking Satan, Beth would always pray to Jesus for her healing and tell Him she believed He was going to heal her (see Psalm 107:20). She didn't know when her healing would take place, but she came to believe Jesus had the power to make her well. She also prayed for other people who were suffering from migraine headaches. She then played praise music, knowing how much Satan hates hearing the name of Jesus being glorified. She continued doing this for several hours a day. While she was doing this, she would feel her pain suddenly disappear for a period of time. When it would return, she would again tell Satan to flee (see again James 4:7).

From the Book of Job to Peace

Despite seeing God work in my own body and seeing Beth's pain subside temporarily, I was feeling overwhelmed. I read the book of Job, and it seemed I could fully identify with what Job was going through. At one point I said to someone at church, "How many miracles do I need in my life before it finally sinks in that God loves me?"

I was at the place where I did not know how to pray about the whole situation—Beth's ongoing struggle with pain, her having to live as though she were in a nursing home, the dreaded trips to the pain institute, the financial drain, the uncertainty of our future . . . One day I decided I would say the Lord's Prayer, stating each phrase and then pausing to say what was in my heart related to that phrase. After "Our Father who art in Heaven," I found myself recognizing aloud that God had created me, had sustained me after I was born, and had preserved me. That was as far as I got because I stopped to take in the immensity of what I heard coming out of my mouth. I never even made it to the second phrase of the prayer that day!

I woke up one morning feeling very overwhelmed. I flipped over and lay face down on the bed. I started pounding the pillow out of frustration. I was not praying. I was not, in my mind, seeking out God. As I was pounding the pillow, I heard, *I have heard your prayers, and I am going to heal Beth.*

My response was one word: *When?*

I then heard, *In My time.* With that, a complete sense of peace came over me from the top of my head to my toes.

Back into Life

Meanwhile, Beth never gave up. As the days passed, the length of time the pain stayed away became longer and longer. There were nights as she lay alone in the dark on the couch that she faced torment orchestrated by Satan. She heard a taunting voice telling her that she would never, ever be healed, that God didn't love her, and that she never would be a woman of God. She actually heard sneers. It was during this time that she fully realized that Satan did truly exist, because she saw the expression of his character, which is full of hatred.

Later, there were also nights when she actually heard the Holy Spirit speak to her. His voice was audible. As she heard Him speak, she would feel a sudden sense of peace go throughout her whole body (as I had felt when God spoke to me about His healing her). The Holy Spirit calmed her soul, reassured her, and told her that He would never leave her. "Words cannot not describe the sudden sense of God's presence that I felt," Beth said about that time.

She also said, "A demonic voice and the voice of the Holy Spirit are so different from each other! The voice of Satan or his demons is full of torment and mockery. It brings no peace, only inner turmoil. The Holy Spirit's voice is full of love and compassion. There is calm reassurance in His power." Beth believes that because she heard the Holy Spirit's voice, she had the strength to continue to press on. It was at this time that she finally realized God's power. He gave her the

13. SPIRITUAL SHOWDOWNS, HEAVENLY HEALINGS

strength to believe in His greatness. June 14, 2005, was the last day she had pain, approximately 2½ months after our first meeting with Pastor Bill.

When I was healed before Beth was, she actually felt angry that I had been healed and she had not. She says that now she understands that my healing had to take place first to show her that God had the power to move my bones. By showing her He was willing to move my bones, God was reaching out to her and showing her how much He loves both of us. If He could heal me, He could heal her.

As time passed, Beth got herself back into life again. She regained her strength and stamina much sooner than she expected. After the pain was gone, she knew it was time to get off the couch and act as though she was healed. She wanted to get back into society as soon as possible. She spent the summer riding her bike to get her endurance back. She lost over forty pounds that she had gained from the effects of the steroids she had been prescribed. She got herself back into stores again since she had not been in a store for about a year.

She also did home study courses to keep her nursing license current. This helped her mind start getting used to processing information again. She also had not driven a car for many months and had to get herself behind the wheel again. By August, she was ready to go back to work at the hospital. What a day of rejoicing that was for her! She walked down the hall to the nursing unit where she worked with tears in her eyes. She was overwhelmed by the grace that she had received from God.

That's a Miracle!

In the fall, I had my annual physical with my primary care physician. The nurse took the usual vital sign measurements and told me to put on an examination gown and wait for the doctor. I sat on the end of the examination table.

My doctor of many years knew my history well. Wearing a white lab coat and carrying a clipboard, she came into the exam room and asked, "How are you doing?"

I picked up my feet and looked at them. She peered at my legs and feet over the top of her clipboard and asked, "What?"

I said, "My feet are even."

She looked closer and replied, "That's a miracle! How did that happen?"

I told her about the healing services and how my legs and my shoulders had moved. Hearing that, she got an amazed look on her face.

I went home and read the book of Job again. This time, I began to see what Job had gone through as being extreme and far beyond what I have gone through. I believe that in the healing process, God was healing my memories as well as my body. As we were experiencing God's healing touch, both Beth and I were beginning to move toward a life of health and wholeness.

14

The Testimony Travels

A few months after Beth was healed, one of the elders' wives at church made the comment that she would like something written that she could read to help her understand how Beth got better. Beth decided to write down what she had experienced for the church newsletter. The title of her article was "What Happened to Beth?" Most of the congregation had known something was going on with her, but never knew details of the challenges Beth faced. Before submitting the article, we had a pastor on the church staff review it. He suggested that Beth get up in front of church to explain why she wrote it and to highlight some of the key points in the article. The following is an excerpt from her article, which appeared in the January 2006 edition of the *Cutlerville Contact* (all Scriptures in this excerpt are taken from the NIV 1984).

> As I now look back and reflect on everything I went through, I realize that I actually never had a "migraine headache" but rather a torment of Satan. My warfare was with the devil himself and his demons. My enemy Satan attempted to defeat me with his well laid plans of deception. John 8:44 tells us that Satan is the "father of lies" and II Corinthians 11:14 tells us that "Satan himself masquerades as an angel of light." Satan had lied to me since I was a young girl, and I believed every lie he told me.
>
> While growing up, many events in my life opened the door for the devil's spirits to influence me. And they did. Satan bombarded my mind with nagging thoughts and doubts. These thoughts

played over and over in my mind thousands of times. . . . His plans were well laid; for he had studied me for a long time. He knew all my weaknesses and fears. I was held in bondage due to ways of thinking devised by Satan.

As time passed in my life, he knew exactly how to torment me. It was by having me slowly drop out of life due to pain, believing that God didn't love me, and that God wanted me to suffer. I had gotten Satan and God mixed up. I had believed that God was the originator of suffering instead of the devil. I am now convinced that the devil wanted me to die a slow painful death. After I was better, a friend who would visit me told me that she had been convinced that Satan wanted me dead. She truly thought I was going to die, as did my husband and family.

It was not until I believed John 8:32 that I was able to overcome the devil. This text tells us, "You will know the truth, and the truth will set you free." This was exactly how I was able to have victory over Satan. I replaced all of Satan's lies with the truth, the Word of God. I not only had to study God's Word to know the truth, but I also had to act to be set free. The weapons I used to defeat Satan were not only the Bible, but also praise and prayer. Praise to God is essential in defeating the devil. Prayer is humbling myself, coming to God asking for help, and talking to him about all my needs.

Before I could be healed, I had to know that Jesus is my friend and that He is with me all the time. I had to know that only He can supply my every need. Jesus used the Word of God to defeat the devil. Whenever Satan would lie to Jesus, Jesus responded with "It is also written" (Matthew 4:7) and quoted him The Word. The joy and freedom which I now have in my life is indescribable. God has released me from all the chains with which Satan bound me. II Corinthians 3:17 states "Now the Lord is the Spirit, and where the Spirit of the Lord is, there is freedom."

Some days I can hardly comprehend what has happened to me. When I started to pursue spiritual healing, the only faith I had was to let Steve put me in the car and show up at the meeting. My faith was gone, and I had lost all hope. It wasn't having enough faith that healed me; it was what Jesus did on the cross that healed me. The New Testament version of Isaiah 53:5 is I Peter 2:24, which says, "He himself bore our sins in his body on the tree, so that we might die to sins and live for righteousness; by his wounds you have been healed." As this verse says, Jesus not only died to pay for my sins, He also accomplished my healing while He was on the cross. I have truly, without a doubt, been healed by Jesus' wounds. My life verse has become, "For you, O Lord, have delivered my soul from death, my eyes from tears, my feet from stumbling, that I may walk before the Lord in the land of the living" Psalm 116:8–9.

Beth spoke the same Sunday the newsletter was handed out. The next day, one of my mother's friends called her. She said her daughter-in-law attended a church fifteen miles away, and that Monday morning someone attending a Bible study with her daughter-in-law had brought a copy of Beth's testimony to the Bible study. The woman who brought the newsletter was excited to share Beth's story.

A few weeks later, we were shopping in a department store and happened upon an elderly woman we had not seen in a few years. She had been our neighbor when I was growing up, and I had spent a lot of time at her house, playing with her kids during my junior high years. She had several relatives who attended our church. She reported that at a family reunion, one of her relatives told her the senior men from our church who met at the donut shop got into quite a discussion about what Beth had said and written. She said most of them had reached the consensus "we'll see how long that lasts." She also said, "I told him if Steve said he was healed, it's true. If it were anyone else, I wouldn't have believed it!"

Tapering Off by Faith

Our final visits to the doctor at the neurological institute compelled us to continue trusting in God. We believed that Beth had the root cause of her issue leave her, and that she had been taught how to deal with spiritual affliction. With the source of pain gone, the side effects of the drugs Beth was on for treatment intensified. She wanted to be taken off the drugs.

The doctor's first response to Beth being pain free was, "You are still having the headaches; they are just controlled." At this point, she was on high doses of several medications to "control" her pain. To minimize current and long-term side effects, the clinic's goal was to reduce the number of these drugs once a patient had stabilized. At an earlier visit, the doctor had asked Beth to start thinking about which drug she felt might not be helping. Beth brought this up again, and he said they wanted patients to be stable for at least six months before reducing their drugs. He asked what she was thinking. She wanted to get off all of the drugs, but for a start she said, "Well, anything I am still on that was prescribed before I came here wasn't working."

The doctor took a look at her and asked, "You've had no headaches?" His idea of pain control was getting bad days down to five to ten days a month. He was taken aback when Beth told him she had no pain. He then sat down and began to write the drug reduction schedule for several drugs. One by one, she was tapered off them.

Three months later, on the way to the next visit, Beth and I were discussing how to convince the doctor to take her off the last medications he himself had prescribed—the drugs he said were now "controlling" the pain. We came up with a well-rehearsed approach. When we got into Beth's appointment, however, I couldn't believe what she said to the doctor. It wasn't what we had planned! She told the doctor, "I've been to a place called the Healing Rooms, and I've gotten to the bottom of the reason for the pain."

The doctor slowly said, "You know you are taking a risk."

"It's a risk I'm willing to take," replied Beth.

He wrote her another drug reduction schedule. Coming off these final drugs was a real test of our faith because removing them from her system caused side effects too. One drug in particular (the one that could have caused severe health issues if Beth ate overripe fruit) was a drug that very few patients had ever been taken off, so the doctors had limited information on how to taper off the dosage. In coming off this drug, Beth experienced severe heart palpitations, shortness of breath, nausea, and fatigue.

As soon as Beth completed being tapered off that drug, she took off the medical alert bracelet. I had once stared at that bracelet and wondered if our situation were permanent. A few weeks later, I spotted the bracelet lying in a back corner of the kitchen counter. I said, "We need to get rid of that!" I took it to my workshop, bent it over, and flattened it with a hammer.

Beth was off all medication by February 2006, but it took several months for her heartbeat to stabilize. She does fine now and has not been on any medication for over fifteen years.

At her final visit to the neurological institute, Beth told the psychologist what she had been taught at the Healing Rooms and described what she had gone through to get better. She was surprised by his response. He said, "You took what you were taught by those people and you did it. Most of my patients don't take what I tell them outside the walls of this facility."

One of the elders at church came up to me one Sunday and said, "I read Beth's article. I can kind of understand what happened to Beth. But you . . ." He shook his head as he walked away. He wasn't denying what had happened to me. In fact, he knew my history and could see the change. He was simply expressing that what had happened was something beyond his understanding. For years after this, when we would cross paths with this man he would smile and ask us how Beth was doing. We would tell him Beth was doing great, and he would shake his head a bit and get a bigger smile on his face.

Where We All Belonged

When the day came to bring Anna to college, she got out of bed and we packed the van. Before we left, I looked into Anna's room and saw the unmade bed just as she left it. I thought, *She won't be sleeping in that bed tonight.*

The drive was fairly stressful. There was quite a bit of traffic backup going into the Chicago area. Once at the school, we wheeled all her things into her dorm room. That evening, the college had a meet-and-greet for parents, students, and staff in an outside picnic atmosphere. Toward the end of the event, Beth and I observed several parents giving their kids long hugs and walking away teary eyed. One lady started to sob.

Anna was with a few other girls when she came up to us and said, "I'm going back to the dorm with my suite mates. I'll see you a little later."

We said to her, "We should be going."

"Okay," she replied, and Beth and I each gave her a quick hug and watched her walk back to her dorm.

On the walk back to the car, we reflected on how this was different for us than for many of the other parents. We knew Anna was where she belonged. We knew God had enabled Beth to go back to work and, in that way, had provided for us. With His care, we were able to help Anna get started on her collegiate adventure, and as a couple we were on a path to getting back to where we belonged too. God was restoring what Satan had for so long been in the process of stealing from our family and our health. We all were so grateful for where He was taking us next.

15

For Us and for Our Children . . .

One Saturday, I stopped into the Healing Rooms to pick up some of their brochures so I could hand them out to people. One of the leaders gave me a short stack. He started chatting with me about the possibility of having Beth and me volunteer at the Healing Rooms. He said, "With what you have gone through, it seems God would want to use you in some type of healing ministry."

I was feeling underqualified to be a volunteer. My response was, "For now, I see us as a referral service to tell people about what God does through the Healing Rooms."

He and I chatted a bit about hearing from God in order to know what He wanted us to do. My question for him was, "How do we know if something is from God, or is just what we would consider a logical conclusion?"

He answered, "Sometimes God tells us things about people who come into the Healing Rooms. He only tells us what we need to know. Would you like us to go to God and see what He has for you?"

To make me more comfortable, he further explained that most of the time it was a single word that was revealed. (This is the gift of a word of knowledge, one of the spiritual gifts the Bible mentions in 1 Corinthians 12:4–11.) He also said, "Many times, the application or meaning is only known to the person being prayed for."

"I'm open to that," I told him.

He and I went into the room where the volunteers gathered in the moments when they weren't needed to pray for someone directly. There were two volunteers available. The leader who had met me at the door told them what he intended to do. He prayed, and the three of them took some time to hear from God. One of the volunteers then made the statement, "Something is stirring in you that was planted long ago."

I thought, *Okay, whatever.* Another volunteer wrote what had been heard on a card for me. I accepted the card, thanked them for their time, and left. I pondered the statement a bit, but it would be many years before what it referred to would hit me. When it did, it was very powerful.

Enough Faith in God's Plan?

Our son Eric was in his first year of varsity football a year after Beth was healed. He hurt his knee at practice one day. He hobbled around a bit, but played on Friday night. A couple of times, he stopped short on the field and favored his leg. I was concerned, but after the game he came home and ran down the steps to his room. I thought, *Looks like he's okay.*

But he was not okay. He had an ACL tear in his knee. We were told he needed surgery. We brought Eric to the Healing Rooms, and volunteers prayed for him. We had made plans to visit our daughter Anna, who was doing a semester in Spain. Eric's surgery was scheduled the very morning Beth and I were leaving for Spain.

After our own healings, we were wondering why God didn't simply work an immediate miracle on Eric, but rather allowed him to go through having to deal with this type of injury. We brought him to the surgical center. We were still thinking that when the surgeon went to work, he would find a normal knee and Eric would be spared surgery and rehabilitation.

My parents drove to the surgical center as well because they were going to take Eric home and care for him until we returned from Spain. We put our son in God's hands and left as planned. That evening between connecting flights, we called my parents. They reported that the surgeon had repaired the damage and Eric was doing fine. He would need to be on crutches for an extended period of time and go through rehab. I felt let down at that report and began to wonder if we should have prayed more or if we really didn't have faith.

When we were in Spain, we went to the palace in Madrid. We stayed in Seville, where we saw the tower where Columbus had docked his boat prior to leaving for the New World. We visited some Roman ruins and went to the beach in the area Jonah was running away to when God had told him to go to Nineveh. We had a great time, but all the while Eric's situation was on my mind. Many evenings when we were in Spain, I was wrestling with how things had turned out for Eric.

When we got home, Eric was up to using his crutches to get into his car and drive himself to school. After a few days, an infection set into his knee. Beth took him to the doctor, and Eric was told to keep his leg elevated. The nurse told him, "I don't want you going to the game tonight and standing on the sideline in the damp air with your leg hanging down."

That day, Eric's coach asked him how he was doing and Eric showed him the infection in his leg. As much as Eric wanted to be at the game, he chose to stay home.

The man who originally hosted Pastor Bill Putnam had arranged for him to come back to town to minister. The weekend Eric had the infection was the same weekend Pastor Bill was coming to town. We asked Eric if he wanted to go to one of the meetings, and Eric said he would like to go.

Beth called the man hosting the meetings. He said, "Pastor Bill just pulled in. Why don't you let him get settled, and then bring Eric here this evening?" Pastor Bill lived over a thousand miles away. It was a long drive, so he deserved some time to settle in!

Eric wasn't feeling well. He had vomited a couple of times that day and wasn't interested in food. We put a mattress in the back of our van for him, and he rode lying down as we took him to see Pastor Bill. When we arrived at the house, Eric used his crutches to get into the family room and lie on the host's couch. We interacted with Pastor Bill for a bit. Then he walked over to Eric, put his hand on Eric's leg, and said, "I curse the infection in this leg and tell it to be gone, in Jesus' name."

The infection was the only need we were aware of, but Pastor Bill then lightly touched the Achilles tendon in the affected leg and said, "I speak to this tendon, in Jesus' name, and tell it to lengthen out."

We could see Eric's foot rotate as his toes moved to a position where they were pointing to the ceiling. His toes had moved about an inch and a half. Then we had no more than left when Eric said, "I'm hungry!" We pulled into McDonalds and bought him two burgers.

The next morning, Beth unwrapped the bandage on Eric's leg. The infection was completely gone. All she could see were the two marks left from the surgery. Later in the week, we told Pastor Bill how quickly it went away, and even he was surprised at how quickly Eric had been healed of the infection. It was a miraculous, although progressive, healing with more steps to come.

Knowing Eric tended to be a private person, I said to him, "You don't need to tell everyone about this, but if someone asks you what happened, you can't deny it. You need to tell them."

Eric went to school thinking, *How do I tell these people about this?* The football coach asked him how he was doing, which gave him an opening. Eric showed him his leg and then told him about being prayed for and how quickly his infection had gone away.

When it came time for Eric's rehab process, the physical therapist put him on an exercise bike. "Let's see how far around you can turn the pedal," she said.

Eric was able to make the complete revolution, which surprised the physical therapist. He still needed to work on range of motion and strengthening, but he had a good head start. Rehab went well and didn't take as long as expected.

Years later, Eric shared with me that he had reflected on his healing many times. He said it was the first time in his life he had really felt the power of God.

16

New Teachings, New Habits

The church we were attending when Beth's healing took place held morning services at a different location for a few weeks while the sanctuary was being renovated. Members were encouraged to attend another church for the evening service. One Sunday evening, Beth and I visited a large independent Full Gospel church. The pastor had come from the same denominational background as I had. We knew that this church held healing services, and after hearing rumors from people who didn't attend there, we expected healing to be the main focus. We were surprised that healing wasn't mentioned in the service. We started attending Saturday evening services there regularly, and it was a few weeks before healing was mentioned directly. We thought that was a good thing because we didn't want to get involved with a church where the goal was a bigger miracle this week than last week.

For several months, we attended our denominational church both Sunday services and the Full Gospel church on Wednesday and Saturday nights. Soon we began to realize that if we were to grow in the areas God was leading us toward, we should become members at the Full Gospel church. We decided to meet with one of the leaders of the church we were planning to leave. We told him why we were leaving and that we had no hard feelings. We told him that if the congregation needed anything done that we were uniquely qualified for, he could call us. He responded by telling us if we thought God wanted us at different church, we should go.

Praying beyond the Past

One of the teachings we heard early on at our new church concerned forgiveness. My understanding of the teaching goes like this: When we are hurt or offended by someone and hold things against the person for what he or she did, we are actually allowing what was said or done to us to continue to have power over us. Forgiving doesn't mean we are saying that what was done was not an issue. In forgiving, we say we are not going to hold bitterness against the person who created the offense, and we are giving it to God. Part of giving it to God is praying for the person who created the offense and asking God to reach out with His love to that person.

Learning about that, I began to wonder if I still needed to forgive the kids from my junior high for the way they had treated me concerning my sports abilities (or lack thereof, due to the brace and the resulting physical challenges). I didn't think I had any lingering resentment toward them, but I had never prayed for them.

I dug into my filing cabinet and pulled out the graduation program from junior high. I went into a private place and opened the program. There was a separate picture of each person. When I looked at the first picture, the hurts that person had experienced in our childhood years came to my mind. I prayed that through the power of God, that person could overcome the effects of what had happened.

I moved on to the second person, and the issues that person had to deal with when younger came to mind. I continued going through the pictures. Into my mind would come an understanding of what struggles each person had, and I prayed for him or her. For some of these people, the things that came to mind were issues later in their lives. I now believe it was the Holy Spirit bringing these things to mind so I could pray for each person specifically.

Something came to mind for every last person in my class. This showed me that I had considered my challenges greater than what other people had to face. I realized now that this was not true. My challenges may have been different, but living in a fallen world, with Satan coming against us to steal, kill and destroy, affects all of us.

At the new church, we were presented with another simple but very powerful teaching that relates to forgiveness: Everything we say either feeds the Kingdom of God or the kingdom of Satan. This really helped me understand what happened in junior high. The kids were feeding the kingdom of Satan and not realizing it. I know that I am not always feeding the Kingdom of God with my words either, even now.

God Gives Back More

One Wednesday night service, a guest speaker spoke on the topic of tithing. He spoke of how God has a way of making our 90 percent go farther when we tithe than 100 percent goes when we don't tithe. He also emphasized that tithing leads to a closer walk with God because we are giving the firstfruits to God and learning to trust Him.

Beth and I discussed the option of tithing, and I did what a person shouldn't do in this situation. What you should do is simply jump in, start tithing, and trust God that what He says in His Word is real. What I did was get out our calculator. I reviewed our family budget and then said to Beth, "It will be tight, but I think we can do it." So we started tithing.

A few months later, Beth left for work early one morning to make sure she had time to give a gift card to a co-worker in need. At an intersection near our house the traffic light turned red. She put her foot on the brake, but the van kept going. There was a thin layer of black ice in the intersection, and the antilock brakes didn't sense any one of the wheels gripping the road. She hit a car, and our van spun around and ended up jumping a curb. No one got hurt. We had an older van on which we had dropped the full coverage insurance. It took about $600 to get the van back on the road.

Then we found out that our insurance policy hadn't been set up to cover the deductible for the person Beth had hit. This coverage was just a few dollars a year, and our insurance company hadn't caught the fact that it never had been added to our policy. That oversight cost us another $500 to do the right thing and pay that person's deductible. It was almost as if Satan was screaming in our ear, *You want to start tithing and helping people out? It's going to cost you eleven hundred dollars!*

We kept on tithing.

The next summer, Anna took a class at our local community college to use up a portion of her remaining state scholarship money that had to be used in-state. Even with taking this class, there would be scholarship money left over that she wouldn't use and would consequently end up forfeiting. A few weeks after her class ended, we got a check in the mail from the college for several hundred dollars. The notation on the check stated that it was to cover the cost of books and room and board. I called the college to see what was going on and told them Anna was living at home that summer. They said the state recognized the full cost of her education regardless and had issued a check for the balance of her scholarship. The college was refunding us the balance!

We also had a few other incidents where money came to us unexpectedly that summer. The total amount of unexpected money was a couple of hundred dollars more than the car accident had cost us. Later, we crossed paths with the guest speaker who had spoken on tithing. We related to him our experience with the accident and how more unexpected money came in than what the accident had cost us. His reply was, "That's the way it works. God provides for us in unexpected ways. He gives us back more than it costs us to tithe."

God Grows Out My Bones

God gives us what He knows we need, when we need it. I have experienced further healing over time. Beth and I went to a conference on spiritual healing where at the close of one session, the speaker had people in need of further healing line up. Those of us who responded stood side by side at the entry to the auditorium to have hands laid on us. I was near the center of the line, watching what was happening.

Just about every other person in the line was blanking out and being helped to the floor.

When I had seen things like this on television, I had always thought they were staged. The speaker was moving quickly down the line. He touched my forehead, and things went dark. The next thing I knew, I was lying on the floor and thinking, *I wonder what that's all about?* Yet after experiencing my bones moving dramatically in ways I had never seen before, my mind was open to seeing God move in more ways I had never seen.

A few days after the conference, I noticed an unusual sensation above and below my knee, and in the ankle of the leg with the shorter bone lengths. It felt like growing pains. I started putting a carpenter's level across my kneecaps to see if my knees were leveling out. The bubble would shoot off to one side. One day a few weeks later, I was speaking on the phone with Pastor Bill and asked him, "Do you think God is growing out my bones?"

He answered, "It very well could be. I can pray over you again, or someone else can. It doesn't matter who."

Beth and I had been attending a short series of classes presented by a ministry focused on teaching about spiritual freedom in Jesus. As we took in what we were taught, time and time again we would recognize how what we had already experienced was explained in the Bible. At the next session we went to, I had the leaders pray over me for physical healing and I ended up on the floor again. When I sat up, an older man in the room said, "When you were on the floor, I could see your feet moving."

This was the second time I had walked away from a meeting while trying to keep my balance. When we got home, I put the level across my knees and the bubble was right in the middle. My leg bones had grown in my shorter leg!

Seek Out God, Not Us

About two years after her healing, Beth and I became volunteers at a healing ministry at our church. Over the years, we have been privileged to pray with many people. We consider it a responsibility to approach serving in this capacity properly. People who come in for prayer are God's children. They are not projects. They are of infinite worth. We believe they are seeking out God and not us. We have come to believe that we are to point out the truth of God's Word to them and stand with them in prayer.

Before we meet with someone, we pray that the Holy Spirit will show us any special prayer needs the person coming in has. Our goal is to bring to that person what God wants brought to him or her. We have seen some dramatic things happen, but the purpose is to lift up, build up, and cheer up in the Lord.

In addition to the healing ministry, there have been times over the years that Beth has had opportunities to pray with patients at the hospital. She has been a nurse in a digestive disease unit for many years, and frequently patients have initiated conversations using the terms *God* or *church*. There are times when Beth has shared part of her story and it has resulted in a patient asking her to pray with him or her.

When these opportunities have arisen in the course of Beth's workday, she has waited to pray over patients until after she clocks out at the end of her shift. That way, she hasn't taken time from her employer to do it. Several dramatic healings have taken place when she has ministered to patients in this way. The most common thing, however, and probably the most important, is that after hearing Beth's story many patients go on to really seek out God on their own.

17

God Is God, and We Are Not

As time passed, Beth and I were given more opportunities to share our story with people we didn't know. We also were growing in dealing with our challenging thoughts and experiencing further healing. Best of all, we were receiving excellent advice and teaching on praying for people.

Beth's parents would winter just north of Bradenton, Florida. One time, her mother shared our story with one of the ladies at the church she and Dad were attending. We were asked to talk to their Bible study about our experiences the next time we visited.

The next winter, we flew into Fort Myers and stayed with my parents for a few days before driving north to Bradenton to see Beth's parents. The night before we were to leave my parents' place, I experienced a severe pain in my chest and immediately thought, *Something doesn't want us to head north.* I said to Beth, "I feel as if I'm having a heart attack. But what are the odds of that happening right now?"

We prayed about it and then told Satan to stay away from us, in Jesus' name. I was still in discomfort but eventually went to sleep. I had a dream that two men came to me to explain the reason for the chest pain. When I woke up, I couldn't recall most of the details of what was said in the dream, but the pain was gone.

Beth and I had an uneventful drive to Bradenton. When we arrived at her parents' church for the Bible study, the pastor was there, as was the person who had invited us, along with about a dozen other people. We shared our story and answered a few questions. After we finished, one of the people shook his head and said, "You're just ordinary people! I grew up in a church that taught about divine healing, but we didn't see it happen. We came to believe that you have to be good enough to have God heal you. I just can't get over the fact that you're just ordinary people!"

When we were leaving, another person said, "When someone comes to speak and isn't passing a collection plate, you know that person came for the right reason!"

A Festering Thought

At one point, this thought crossed my mind: *It sure would have been nice if, when I found out I had to wear the brace, someone had cared enough to pray for me the same way Pastor Bill did.* Sometimes passing thoughts can go down a bad path. The more I thought about it, the more I began to feel let down by the local religious leaders of my youth who had not had an answer for me at the time. I never confronted anyone about it, but an attitude was festering in me.

The church I grew up in didn't teach about expecting recognizable divine healings or miracles to take place in modern times. This church recognized that the Holy Spirit existed, but very little was written in its doctrines about Him. A couple of years after Beth and I were married, I had started to wonder more about the Holy Spirit. I had attended Christian school and had been in church doctrine classes, so I thought I knew quite a bit about the Father and the Son. But I really knew nothing significant about the Holy Spirit. When I asked a pastor where I could learn more about the Holy Spirit, his response was, "There isn't much written about the Holy Spirit from the perspective of our religious tradition. The reason is that the doctrines were formulated in response to perceived heresies. The proper view of the Holy Spirit wasn't being contested at the time the doctrines were written."

As I prayed more about the situation, I realized that the local religious leaders had done what they could at the time, with what they knew. They hadn't ever experienced the fuller picture of seeing people being directly healed by the power of God, so of course at that difficult time when I was facing wearing the brace, they had not come and prayed over me in the same manner as Pastor Bill had so many years later.

Still, I knew things could have gone differently for me way back then. Would it even have been possible for God to reach out to me without someone like Pastor Bill being involved? My answer came from a source I didn't expect. Our house needed a new roof, and Beth and I decided it was a good time to have the chimney rebuilt. Someone put us in touch with two brothers who were from a family of multigenerational brick layers. These guys had a reputation for excellent craftsmanship and worked on a lot of high-end new construction.

When one of the brothers came out to give us an estimate, he told me they were scheduling jobs several weeks out. He made the comment that God had been sending a lot of business their way. That started us on a rambling conversation about God. I told him about Beth being healed of migraines. He replied, "When I was a kid, I had bad migraines for a couple of years. One night when I was eight, I was praying before I went to sleep. I said, *God, let's take care of this.* The next morning, the pain was gone and hasn't come back."

What hit me was that when I was ten and was facing wearing the brace, I could have done the same as he had done. I had my Bible back then. I was familiar with the same healing Scriptures that the Healing Rooms had given us later. I could pray. I had everything I needed to bring my situation to God on my own. Would God have done the same miracle at that time as He did thirty-four years later? I don't know. What I do know is that I couldn't blame another human for my having been in my situation for so long.

Softening Scar Tissue

Another year when Beth and I were in Florida for a week, we rented a canoe at Lovers Key State Park along the Gulf. We paddled into a backwater connected to the inlet that wound around to an eventual dead end. We were turning around when a dolphin surfaced next to us. It starting going in the same direction as we were.

We would paddle, and the dolphin would surface to get air and go back under. We would guess where it would surface next. Sometimes we would hear it blow air before we saw it. We had to paddle a bit faster than normal to keep up with it.

When we reached the inlet, the dolphin headed toward open water. Beth and I sat in the canoe and watched it go. Suddenly, it turned around and headed back toward us. We were in about eighteen inches of water. The dolphin appeared to be about a third of the way out of the water. It was swimming fast enough that water was flowing over the top of its head. It looked like a torpedo heading for our canoe!

Beth and I were ready to go swimming if the dolphin tipped us over. That dolphin only missed the front of the canoe by a foot! It then headed in the direction of the canoe rental stand. We kept up with the dolphin all the way back.

When we got back to where we staying, my side hurt from scar tissue tightness, but not any more than it had from time to time in the past. I was lying on the bed and said to Beth, "Come pray over my side."

She came over and put her hand over the incision line on my side and prayed. My side went cold and numb under her hand. She said with a reverent, yet astonished tone of voice, "I can feel things happening to your scar tissue."

Beth later said that the lumps of decades-old scar tissue felt like hard popcorn kernels exploding as they popped. My side was significantly softened up afterward. She had prayed over my side many previous times. Why this softening took place on this particular day, I cannot explain.

Learning More from Pastor Bill

For several years, the man who hosted Pastor Bill Putnam would arrange twice a year for him to come back to minister. The number of people attending the meetings continued to increase, making it necessary to move to a bigger venue. Local churches started opening their doors.

Pastor Bill's healing services continued in the same format. There was an opening teaching, an invitation for salvation, and the actual healing service. He would have several chairs in front of him where people would come forward and sit. He would be seated in a chair on wheels, and he would pray for the person in the chair at the end of the line, and then roll his way over to the next chair. At times, he would pause to tell a story of a healing or do some teaching relative to the prayer needs he had just addressed.

At one of the services, an evangelist who had a real heart for the lost and had started several churches in our region attended to see what was happening. I recall the look of astonishment on his face as he observed Pastor Bill praying over a lady's shoulders and God moving her arms. She was holding her hands out and she had dark red fingernail polish on, so it was easy to see that her hands were moving.

At another service, a lady was in a wheelchair. She was very emotional. She said to Pastor Bill, "I came for prayer the last time you were here, but God hasn't healed me!"

Pastor Bill spoke to her a bit about how God loved her despite the circumstances. He then asked his wife, Melva, to get up, telling us all, "My wife has a hugging ministry." His wife hugged the lady for a long time. Afterward, the lady appeared much more peaceful.

Six months later, at his next visit, a lady in a wheelchair came up to be prayed for. She raised herself up out of the wheelchair and stood with a beaming smile on her face. She was the same lady! She looked so different that at first I didn't recognize her. She gave a report: "My physical therapist thought I would never walk, but I can take some steps. Praise God!"

Pastor Bill's response when he heard that was, "This is an excellent example of a healing in which God moves over time."

Pastor Bill would have a slightly different focus in his teaching time each night. There were at least two times over the years when his teaching focused on how scientists were discovering that babies are aware of what happens to them before they are born and how this affects us long-term. He pointed out Scriptures related to the scientific findings, referencing how God forms us in our mother's womb and how John the Baptist leapt in Elizabeth's womb when Mary approached (see Psalm 139:13; Luke 1:41). Each time he taught on this, I was left with the impression that there was something deeper in that teaching for me, but I didn't know exactly what.

At the end of one of these services, after everyone left, I went to the front of the church and approached Pastor Bill. We were sitting in chairs facing each other. At this point, we were well acquainted. I pointed to my left side and said, "I'm doing a lot better, but the scar line itself still has a burning sensation."

He closed his eyes and nodded a bit. Then he leaned forward, put his hand on my side, and said, "I speak to the nerve endings the surgeon cut that are not supposed to be firing and tell them to be silenced, in Jesus' name."

Immediately the burning sensation went away. It has not returned.

Pastor Bill was an excellent person to introduce us to the subject of divine healing. He simply pointed us to God's Word. He made the statement, "If you ever hear me say anything that conflicts with what you read in the Word of God, run the other way." One of his foundational teachings was entitled "The Doctrine of Brokenness." In this teaching, he made the statement that at some point everyone needs to be at the place where they realize they are totally broken and cannot fix their own situation and need the salvation of Jesus.

Pastor Bill was quoted in one church periodical, *The Banner*, as saying he regarded himself as an instrument in the Lord's hands, or as an empty fruit jar that God uses to display His power. He stated, "I'm not a faith healer, neither do I believe in faith healing." What he did believe is that God quite often honors the specific prayer request of His people as they pray in faith. "God is sovereign," he went on to say, "and knows what's best for us."[7]

---

7. John Kerssies, "A Gentle Touch of God," *The Banner*, November 20, 2000, 14–17.

Three Kinds of Faith

The article noted that Pastor Bill would point out three kinds of faith in the Bible. The first kind is *trusting faith*. This is faith in Jesus for eternal salvation.

The second kind he pointed out is *obedient faith*. This kind of faith means following the Lord in obedience and doing His will—sometimes against all odds.

The third kind of faith is demonstrated in Acts 3:6, when Peter said to a crippled person, "In the name of Jesus Christ of Nazareth, rise up and walk" (NKJV). Pastor Bill called this *authoritative faith*. When praying with authoritative faith, we are, as Pastor Bill said in referencing Jesus, "speaking to the mountain" (see Mark 11:22–23).

How did Pastor Bill come to understand divine healing? He grew up as a Mennonite on a farm in North Dakota. He was a grocery store manager and at one point worked as a furniture salesman. One evening he was attending a Bible study where James 5:14–15 was the focus: "Is anyone among you sick? Let him call for the elders of the church, and let them pray over him, anointing him with oil in the name of the Lord. And the prayer of faith will save the sick, and the Lord will raise him up" (NKJV). Afterword, he was talking with another man in the Bible study and they were asking themselves if they *really* believed what the Scripture said. They purchased a small bottle of vegetable oil and went to visit a man with terminal cancer from their town. He was in the hospital, and during their visit they said to him, "The Bible says we should pray for you and anoint you with oil in the name of the Lord, and He will raise you up. Would you like us to do that?"

The man said, "Go ahead—it won't hurt. I'm going to die anyway."

Pastor Bill said he had no idea how much oil they should use, but he recalled the oil running down Aaron's beard in the Bible (see Psalm 133:2), so he poured the entire bottle over the man when they prayed!

It was several days before both men could return to the hospital together. When they did, they knocked on this patient's door and there was no response. They opened the door and looked inside. They saw an empty bed, and their first thought was that he had died.

They went to the nurse's station and inquired about him. The nurse said, "It was the strangest thing. A couple of days after you were here, we couldn't find anything wrong with him and sent him home."

This experience led Pastor Bill to seek out God in the areas of healing and deliverance from demonic oppression. He spent many years as a traveling evangelist and eventually became the pastor of two churches. He recorded a teaching for people in ministry in which he made the statement, "Check my office anytime; you will find only one book. A Bible. I've looked into some of the commentaries, and there's nothing wrong with some of those, but God told me to stick with the Book and He would give revelation."

God would give Pastor Bill revelation in some interesting ways. For example, early in his ministry he thought a person had to be saved to be divinely healed. He found out that was not the case. At one of his healing services, an entire family came forward for prayer. Each person had a significant medical challenge. Every family member had a dramatic healing that evening, which Pastor Bill found to be quite unusual. The next evening when he gave the altar call, the entire family came forward to be saved.

Pastor Bill shared with us that he started to have so many people coming to him that he didn't have enough time to spend with each person. So he asked God to show him exactly what was happening in the lives of the people coming to him so he could pray quickly and directly for the issues that were affecting them. There were many times we sat and watched as he ministered to a person he had never met before. He would bring up specific incidents from that person's past, and the person would sit there amazed. In some cases, he would explain to a person what was going on in the spirit world, and he would bind and break a spirit affecting that person. Then he would speak healing and peace into their life.

Pastor Bill shared another important thing at one of his teaching times that Beth and I always try to remember. He stated, "When you start praying authoritative prayer and God starts moving, remember God is God and you are not."

18

Having an Influence on Our World

Over the years, I've been given opportunities to reach out to people from my past whom I had not seen for many years. Or, perhaps more accurately, God has been reaching out to them through my story.

One of the first times this occurred was shortly after our daughter Jan graduated from high school. She and I were picking up a few things in the mall when I crossed paths with one of my junior high classmates. I had not seen him for many years. As we were catching up by sharing our life experiences, I shared the story of God straightening my spine. His response was, "Sometimes it's just a matter of how big you let your God be."

A few years later, Beth and I heard that another of my junior high classmates was diagnosed with cancer that was progressing. I was concerned about his situation, but I didn't call him because I was struggling with what I would say to him. I knew I had experienced more than one miracle in my life, but who was I to promise him a miracle?

At one point Beth crossed paths with one of his family members, who told her, "Have Steve call him." So, I called. He was very happy to get my call. He had heard our story. One of the first things he said to me was, "That's really something, what happened to you!" He then said, "I called Pastor Putnam. He explained to me that God didn't intend for me to have cancer when He created me!" From the tone of his voice, you would have thought he had been told that he was cured of cancer and had been given a million dollars too.

This classmate passed away a few weeks later. On the way to the funeral home I was thinking, *This is going to be awkward. I'm not only still alive, but I've had healing and he passed away. I wonder how his family is going to react to me?*

At the funeral home, the members of his family whom I interacted with smiled at me and gave me big hugs. This event caused me to enter a new stage in my contemplation of God. I was left to wonder why He had given me so much protection.

Broadcasting My Healing

For years, I had a clock radio on the nightstand by the bed. I had it set to one of the local Christian stations. As a rule, I would wake up a few minutes before the radio alarm went off, reach over, turn off the alarm, get up, and be on my way. I could go months without having the radio alarm turn on. One morning I woke up and laid in bed for a few minutes. The clock radio turned on. The DJ said, "It's Groundhog Day. One of my favorite movies is *Groundhog Day*. There's a scene from that movie I like to play over and over. Do you have a scene in your life you would like to play over? Call me at . . ."

I had bought an iPod and no longer routinely listened to the radio, so my thought was, *That's why I stopped listening to Christian radio—because they're doing goofy stuff like this.*

I turned off the radio and got out of bed. I was halfway across the room when I heard, *Call!* I believed that the Holy Spirit was prompting me, and I thought, *Okay* . . . I went to the kitchen, pulled out a phone book, and looked up the number for the radio station. I called and was put through to the DJ. I interacted with him for several minutes, telling him about what had happened to me. At the end of our conversation I said, "Maybe there's something in what I said that you can use."

He replied, "I've recorded everything you said. Are you okay with me using it on the air?"

"Go ahead," I said.

What he put on the air was edited to fit the flow of the program, so this was the conversation that went on the radio:

DJ: Good morning, Steve.

Me: I'm calling relative to your request for scenes you would like to play over.

DJ: Yeah, like the movie *Groundhog Day*.

Me: Well . . . this is a little unusual. At the time I was forty-four years old, I had a healing take place. When I was born, I had cancer in my left side. It was a cancerous kidney. People considered it miraculous I survived because they had gotten a radiation machine at Butterworth Hospital and it was all experimental. I am on the very leading edge of people to survive that. And as a result of that, I have a scar almost halfway around my body. I had a lot of scar tissue and my spine grew very crooked and my legs' lengths were uneven.

When I was forty-four, I actually brought my wife to a healing service for her, and this old pastor said, "What would you like prayer for?" I told him all my bone lengths were fixed and probably not much could be done. He told me to sit back and pick up my feet. He hung onto my feet and said, I'm going to tell the spirit of asymmetry to come out of your body, your hips to soften up and your leg to come down an inch [In Jesus' name]."

And I sat there and watched it do it in about four seconds. So my [spine and] legs are straight. So that's the scene. And to really have that hit you that God wants, and that's the main point too—a lot of times people are like *I need to be healed, I need to be healed*, and we do—and I think God does want to heal us, but sometimes people pursue it just because they want it. But coming to understand the relationship God wants with us is the bigger part of it, even if we're left with something that in our mind isn't totally [corrected.]

We'll run into people and talk to them about these things when we are on vacation or whatever, and that's kind of the message we bring them. You know, it's not just trying to get what we want, but line up with what God wants for us and understand that He loves us, and a lot more of that falls in place than what we think when that happens.

Later that day, our daughter Jan called me. She said she had been listening to the radio that morning and her first thought was, *There's someone out there just like Dad.* Then she realized, *That is Dad!*

The radio station received callers' requests to replay this sound clip again and did so the next day.

Other Healing Stories

One Sunday at the start of one of his visits, Pastor Bill was asked to preach at a Sunday service at one of the churches hosting him that week. We visited this church to hear him preach. As we entered the foyer in the back, one of the women from my high school class spotted us and came up to us. She said, "Everybody's talking about what happened to the two of you!"

The healing services that week were held each evening in the church fellowship hall. The healing portions were structured so that people could come and go a bit. One of the evenings when I came into the room, I saw a high school classmate I hadn't seen since graduation. He was listening intently to Pastor Bill as he was ministering. When my classmate saw me, he loudly whispered, "Hey, Steve!" I stopped and sat down by him. "Look at my hand!" he said.

It looked normal to me. I asked, "What about it?"

He said, "I scraped it up a couple of months ago, and it got infected and wouldn't heal. Pastor Bill prayed for me a couple of days ago, and the wound started crusting over in fifteen minutes. The next day, it was completely healed!"

Several months later, at another one of Pastor Bill's semi-annual visits, the woman who had earlier greeted us before the church service, along with her husband, was asked to get up and tell their story. Her husband said he was an elder at their church, and during the healing services at Pastor Bill's last visit the elders were asked to lay hands on people as Pastor Bill prayed for them. Pastor Bill had told them that they might feel something unusual happen as he prayed.

This elder's wife had come forward to be prayed for on the first day of the meetings. She had sat in one of the five chairs set up for people who wanted prayer. Being a church elder, her husband stood behind her with his hands on her shoulders. She had a condition where before she could function properly in the morning, she had to do a lot of stretching of her hip and leg. This condition was due, at least in part, to having one foot with a flat arch, which affected her posture. She wore an insert that a doctor had created to fit inside her shoe to compensate for her condition.

When it was her turn to be prayed for, she felt a gentle sliding out and loosening of her painful hip. Her husband didn't feel anything. After the prayer, she began to feel that she was more even in her stance. At that point, she decided to believe that she was going to be healed, so she pulled the insert out of her shoe. She showed Pastor Bill the insert and said, "I'm going to keep it out."

Pastor Bill replied, "You're going to be all right!"

Over the next three days, she continued to look at her more even stance and her foot, claiming some Bible verses to keep her healing. She still was experiencing some pain, but she declared that she was "sticking with believing." On the third day, with the pain in her hip very much diminished, she realized that she had been given a creative miracle—an arch in her foot. She shared with the church how much feeling the touch of God in her body did for her comprehension of the reality of how much He loves her.

Graduates Anchored in God

Many years later, when Beth and I arrived at my 40th high school reunion, several women came up to me and gave me a hug. I joked with Beth and said, "You didn't know I was that popular in high school, did you?" I knew these ladies were simply expressing thanks for sharing our story and what God had done for them at one of Pastor Bill's meetings.

At the reunion, it seemed almost everyone whom I interacted with made a comment about the importance of God in his or her life. Many of my classmates had either had healings take place at one of Pastor Bill's services or had discovered the power of the Holy Spirit through seeking God as they went through various circumstances in their lives.

One classmate I spoke with had also been in my junior high class. His wife had passed away from cancer a year before the reunion. As we were talking, he shared that many people he worked with would make mocking comments about his faith. When they had problems in their lives, however, they would come into his office, close the door, and ask to talk. He said when his wife was close to passing away, she told him the main thing she wanted at her funeral was to have the salvation message preached because she knew his co-workers and clients needed Jesus and they would be at the funeral. After sharing that, he looked at me with concern and said, "How is your back was doing?" It was obvious he was a man of compassion.

One other classmate I had contact with every few years told me he also had been a patient of Dr. Johns's. The school yearbook notes this classmate as being an all-American football player, and I never suspected that he had any history of health issues. He shared with me that he was given a leukemia diagnosis when he was little. He had memories of being in the pediatric cancer ward when he was four years old and making friends with other patients, only to see some of his new friends pass away. This man had become involved in praying for healing and was also involved in deliverance ministry. He even became heavily involved in orphanage ministry in third-world countries.

The Christian high school we graduated from was founded on the same doctrinal principals as the denomination I grew up in. Our parents sent us to the school with the intention of doing what they could to help us know about God, the way Proverbs 22:6 says: "Train up a child in the way he should go, and when he is old he will not depart from it" (NKJV).

One of the first pages of the yearbook from my senior year contains the following:

> Reflection of a school.
> Whose anchor is secured in the Word.
> Whose peace comes from Christ's death on the cross.
> Whose training and learning are applied by the Spirit.
> Whose graduates will in some way
> Have an influence on the world.

Whoever wrote that was more prophetic than he or she ever imagined. God was not only fulfilling our parents' desire for my classmates and me; He was also providing for our needs and even showing us things about Himself in ways our parents had never expected.

19

He Was There All the Time

ONE DAY, I HEARD SOMEONE BEING INTERVIEWED ON A LOCAL Christian radio station. This person made the statement that the best day of his life was the day he was saved. A thought shot into my mind: *What was the most influential church service of my life?* Immediately, my mind flashed back to the Pentecost Sunday service in the little white church when I was four years old. Then very quickly, the memory of "*something is stirring in you that was planted long ago*" came to me. This was the word spoken over me years before, when a volunteer wrote it on a card and handed it to me at the Healing Rooms.

God was showing me that a mustard seed of faith had been planted in me that Pentecost day. I was in wonderment over all the years that had passed since that Pentecost service. God had worked physically astonishing miracles for me, starting with my birth (and who knows how much before I was born). I knew that, yet I had held Him at arm's length for a long time.

I thought it would be interesting to determine what date Pentecost had fallen on that year, so I researched the actual date. Another thought popped into my head: *The day I was pounding the pillow out of frustration as an adult must have been close to forty years after that Pentecost service.* I had made note of how many days had passed between the day I heard from God *I'm going to heal Beth . . . in My time* and the day Beth walked out of that dark room. I did the math. I had been pounding the pillow forty years *to the day* after that Pentecost service!

Another train of thought then popped into my head. The Children of Israel spent forty years in the wilderness because they trusted the report of the spies who advised them to trust in what they saw, not in what God said was the actual reality. Yet God provided for their needs anyway by keeping their clothes from wearing out and by providing manna for them. I thought, *God has also been providing for me and protecting me, despite my lack of proper response to His care.*

I started to reflect further on the spiritual parallels between the Israelites' experience and mine. I believe I had a proper view of God when I was four years old—much more accurate than the view I adopted as I was growing up and facing all those physical challenges. Even at the age of four, I already knew God had done mighty things to preserve me physically. Perhaps this could be compared to the Israelites being in awe of God when He delivered them from the Egyptians by parting the Red Sea so they could cross over?

In my high school years, however, I was filtering everything I had been taught from the Bible through my own view of the world. As a result, I had developed my personal theology of describing God as the detached bus driver and me as the kid bounced around in the back of the bus. Could this be like the Israelites trusting the reports of what the spies had seen and subsequently wondering why God had left them out in the wilderness?

I know now that God sustained me not only in my early life, but also all the way through. The medical trauma of my early days, and being brought through the trying time with the cyst in my hip just before Beth and I were married, popped into my mind. Next, all the physical healing both Beth and I had experienced since then came to me. Specific incidents that could be considered "near-miss accidents" came to mind. They simply happened, yet we were sustained throughout. The stories I have shared—the fifteen-foot drop from the top of a hill on a snowmobile, the two of us almost walking over a waterfall in the dark, our bear encounter, and me lying under the front of a car in my bike accident—all flashed through my mind.

I believe that God had protected me (and often Beth) in each of these incidents, and He probably had done the same a lot of other times I didn't realize as well. Yes, I was shown I had been in a spiritual wilderness. God was there all the time, taking care of me. And He had more to give me—if I simply asked.

Revisiting My Spiritual Roots

As the years passed, I began to feel a desire to share my story with the congregation I had grown up in. They had outgrown the little white church building on the corner. They sold it in the early 1970s and built a new building in a field a quarter-mile away. The congregation owned a parsonage behind the church, with a parking lot in between. I had never met the current pastor, but I knew that in the past the pastor of that church would typically hold office hours at the church building. A couple of times I put a copy of the little newsletter story "What Happened to Beth?" in my car and said to God, *I'm going to drive around the parking lot of that church. If You want me to interact with the pastor, have him walk across the parking lot when I am coming through.* I made a couple of trips around an empty parking lot, not seeing him.

A few years later, I once again began thinking about that Pentecost Sunday service when I was four. I realized the 50th anniversary of that service was approaching. Out of respect for what the church of my childhood had taught me when I was little, Beth and I attended their evening service on June 6, 2015, on the 50th anniversary weekend of what I consider the most important church service of my life.

Even though word of what had happened to us had gotten around the community, I still had a desire to share it personally with the congregation I had grown up in. I knew, however, that there were some people in the area who didn't believe what had happened to Beth and myself was legitimate, and they saw things from a very different viewpoint than Beth and I did. At the same time, many people did recognize what God had done for us as being legitimate. In order not to create an offense unintentionally, I wasn't going to try to push open any doors in an effort to create an opportunity to share at my childhood church. At the close of the service we attended, I said to Beth, "If no one talks to us afterward, let's just leave." What God did next I consider amazing—truly beyond anything I imagined.

When we got to the back of the church after the service, a lady we knew stopped us and said, "What are you doing here tonight?"

From this lady's tone of voice, I couldn't quite tell if she was happy we were there or not. To me, the situation quickly appeared to be turning awkward, and I thought, *I put us in this position—my desire to attend was my own, and I didn't really ask God if He wanted me to come!* I quickly asked God to help me answer this woman's question without causing offense. I found myself responding by telling her about my experiences in Sunday school and the Pentecost service when I was four, and how what had happened at that service was the mustard seed of faith that led me to the healing meetings and the Healing Rooms. I shared with her how God straightening my spine showed me He is a loving Father. I told her we were attending out of respect for what had taken place so many years ago.

When I told her all that, she quietly said, "The church needs to hear about this. The church's 100th anniversary is coming up soon. A book of remembrances is being put together. You need to talk to one of the people coordinating the book."

We knew these coordinators and spoke to one of them in the parking lot. We shared what had happened to us with him and gave him a copy of "What Happened to Beth?" After we were home, I typed up another page to give them in which I described my early medical history. I also described how when I was growing up, I would see other kids without restrictions and think God must have loved them more than He did me because He had not given them a short leg and a curved spine. I thanked the congregation for praying for me after I was born. I described the impact that the teaching of the Bible stories at Sunday school had on me. I also thanked the church for the reading of God's Word on Pentecost Sunday 1965. I described what had happened at the healing meetings. I detailed how the Word of knowledge at the Healing Rooms showed me that the mustard seed of faith had been planted in me through what had happened in the little white church when I was a child. Through all this, I had come to know God as a loving Father.

What I had written was literally cut and pasted into the church's newsletter so that everyone there could read it. God had provided an opportunity for me to share what He had done for me with that entire congregation, without causing any offense or confrontation. What was particularly meaningful to me was the fact that several members of the congregation were descendants of my Sunday school teachers. Perhaps it had been the Holy Spirit prompting me to attend that church service after all!

10 Things before a Healing

A few years after Beth's healing, she was asked in advance to share her story at one of the services Pastor Bill would be conducting. She agreed to share, but was not sure what to focus on. The night before the service, she prayed for guidance and went to sleep. In the wee hours of the morning she woke up and God impressed her to *"tell them why it took so long."* In the night, she was shown ten concepts she had needed to understand before she was healed:

1. That God loves her (see James 1:17).
2. That God could heal her and overcome unbelief and hardness of heart (see Mark 16:14).
3. That she should allow her husband to be her spiritual head (see Ephesians 5:23).
4. That she was in spiritual warfare, and she personally needed to learn how to fight (see James 4:7; 1 John 4:4).
5. That Satan is a liar and the father of lies. She must replace his lies with the truth (see John 8:32, 44).
6. That the spoken Word of God is powerful (see Romans 10:8).

7. That she should pray for others and get her mind off herself (see Job 42:10; James 5:16).
8. That she should praise God during suffering (see Psalm 34:1–4).
9. That she should humble herself and confess her sins before God (see James 5:16).
10. That she should put to death the old nature—have a metamorphosis by being transformed by the renewing of her mind (see Romans 12:2; 2 Corinthians 10:5; Philippians 4:8; Colossians 3:9).

In her testimony at the service, Beth went into some detail about what it had taken for her to understand these concepts. She made sure it was clear that God had known exactly what her particular situation was, and exactly what she needed not only to be healed but also to thrive long-term. She made the statement that if she would have experienced a miracle at the first healing service she attended, as I did with my spinal curvature, her thought patterns and view of God would have led her back into the same problem. She concluded her presentation with, "My ears had heard of you but now my eyes have seen you" (Job 42:5 NIV).

Beth and I believed God had shown us why it took what we considered a long time for her healing, but even after that we had never been shown what the reason was for the exact amount of time it took. Almost a decade after Beth's talk on "Tell Them Why It Took So Long," we heard Dr. Caroline Leaf, Ph.D., speak. (She is a communication pathologist and cognitive neuroscientist specializing in cognitive and metacognitive neuropsychology.) Dr. Leaf made the statement that when she was in school, the teaching was that our brains are hardwired and could not change. She said that when she read her Bible, however, it said we were to be transformed by the renewing of our mind. She then went into detail about some new discoveries concerning how our thinking patterns affect our brain functions. She had found that when a new concept is introduced, it takes 21 days for a thought to go from short-term to long-term memory. It then takes two 21-day cycles of ingraining the thought before the brain has rewired itself to recognize that thought as normal.

When we heard this, Beth and I turned and stared at each other. The very first service we had attended of Pastor Bill's had been in early April. Until she walked out of the dark room on June 14, she was contemplating what God had done for me, and she was speaking and reflecting on God's Word. As we quickly added up the days Beth had spent renewing her mind, we realized we had just been shown why it had taken until June 14 for her to be healed! The comments Beth had made years earlier about the length of time necessary for her to be healed were now proven out by scientific observation.

A Heart for Understanding

After God showed us why it took a precise amount of time for Beth to be healed, I began to contemplate just how He had preserved me in the early months of my life. I knew that the doctors involved in my care considered my survival a miracle and not simply a medical triumph.

Pastor Bill's teaching on how we are aware of what happens to us before we are born and how it affects us also came back to me. I came to believe that as a newborn I knew in my spirit the method God was using to preserve me, but as an adult, in my mind I could not recall the detail. It could be said that I set my heart to gain understanding, similar to what Daniel did in ancient times. As Daniel was told in Daniel 10:12 (NIV), "Since the first day that you set your mind to gain understanding and to humble yourself before your God, your words were heard . . ."

I won't go into great detail here, but I will say that I know God still fulfills such a request. In a dramatic way, He showed me how He has worked out in my life this biblical promise: "For he will command his angels concerning you to guard you in all your ways; they will lift you up in their hands, so that you will not strike your foot against a stone" (Psalm 91:11–12 NIV). Truly, God's supernatural protection had been provided for me.

20

The Teardrop Trailer Testimonies

After Beth was healed, we got the urge to get away and camp again. The idea of tenting the way we used to do didn't seem appealing. I was browsing the Internet and came across the little teardrop trailers that were popular in the 1940s. These were four by eight feet and contained a bed the size of a sheet of plywood. They were only four feet tall. No standing up! They were really just rolling beds.

It was possible to purchase a new teardrop, but they were handmade and expensive. I found plans to build one but didn't have the time. One day, a person at work spotted a teardrop for sale alongside the road and told me about it. Beth and I went and checked it out. We ended up buying it for less than the price of the material to build one.

We didn't realize what a treasure we had purchased. It turns out our trailer was built by a fourth-generation cabinet builder. It was designed to be pulled behind a classic car to car shows. The trailer was white with a white vinyl roof, and it had a mahogany rack on top. The wheels were outside the body and were enclosed by big, rounded fiberglass fenders that looked as if they had come off a late 1940s car. It even had wide whitewall tires. The trailer's craftsmanship was superb, and it was close to being one of a kind.

The first time we planned on taking the trailer out, we were going to go to Northern Michigan. We got up and checked the weather report. Snow, hail, and tornadoes were predicted for our destination. I said to Beth, "The closest place without rain this weekend is way south of here. Let's go." We got in the van and on the drive debated where to go. By evening, we ended up in a campground we had never been in.

We parked the teardrop and checked out the park. We were sitting in chairs outside the trailer just before bedtime, and it started to rain for a few minutes. We scrambled into the trailer. A few minutes later I realized I had left my Bible on the chair, so I retrieved it. It had gotten wet, and I peeled the pages apart and put it on the overhead shelf in our trailer.

We went to sleep in the 46-inch-wide space. In the morning, I was lying with my back to the wall of the trailer. Beth's knee was in my chest. I reached around her, and there were at least six inches of space between her and the other wall. Beth woke up, stretched, and said, "I slept so good!"

We got up and made breakfast. As we were cleaning up, a lady walked by. She was interested in the trailer and asked how two people could sleep in such a small space. We showed her the inside and talked with her about how Beth had been healed and how we had gotten the trailer so we could start camping again. She asked more questions about what had happened to Beth. We gave her a copy of our story and told her it explained a lot, and we said if she wanted to look at it we could talk more.

Late in the afternoon, we were walking through the campground as we returned from a hike. The door to a trailer opened and the lady we met earlier came out. "I have some questions," she said. "Would you like to come in and talk?"

It appeared she had just finishing cooking something over a fire pit. I commented, "Looks like you're going to eat. Why don't we come back this evening?" We set a time to meet. Beth and I prayed God would give us the right words to speak that evening.

At the agreed upon time, we knocked on the door to her trailer. She invited us in and started asking questions: "Does God do for us everything we ask for?" "How much responsibility is on us if something took place because we didn't go to God soon enough or in the right way?"

As we chatted back and forth, I mentioned my spinal curvature. I said that even though I had lived with it for years and hadn't really gone to God asking for a miracle, God had moved when I finally went to Him. I pointed out that my side still wasn't exactly how I'd like it to be, and that I was learning to trust God to do what He knew was best for my situation.

The lady then shared that an issue had come up earlier in her life and things had not turned out as expected. She was dealing with guilt about the outcome, thinking there was something she might not have done correctly when she was praying about her challenge at the time. She now felt that the resulting situation was her fault.

We interacted a bit, reflecting on the fall of man, the origin of sickness and disease, and the effects of evil on the world. Beth pointed out some lies Satan would have us believe. In this case, Satan wanted this lady to believe the lie that it was her fault that things had not turned out as expected. Satan also didn't want her to realize that he had a hand in the situation. We prayed with her before we left.

The next afternoon, we did some more exploring of the campground. We could see the lady's campsite from where we were. Her entire family had gathered there. They were all out enjoying the weather. That evening, we stopped by their trailer to say good-bye. The lady's husband greeted us at the door. She said she had had a wonderful day and had not felt so free for a long time. Her husband prayed a blessing over us before we left.

Just before we walked away, Beth asked her, "What made you trust us?"

The lady replied, "I saw the Bible open on the shelf over the pillow in your trailer."

It's in the Bible!

One fall, Beth and I were contemplating where to go camping. I had previously noticed a billboard promoting an area that looked interesting, but I couldn't remember the location. A few weeks later, Beth mentioned an area she had been researching that sounded good to her. I checked out the billboard the next time I went by it. Sure enough, it was the same area being advertised. We decided to head in that direction as soon as we got a chance.

One Saturday we hooked up the teardrop trailer and headed out. On the way, Beth mentioned that she had been praying for an opportunity to lead someone to Jesus. As we got close to the campground that was our destination, we started making mental notes of churches we passed so we would know what was in the area when Sunday came.

Even though it was a weekend, the campground had quite a few empty campsites. We set up our trailer and went out for a hike to check out the park. When we got back to the trailer, we found that a motor home had backed into a campsite a little way down from us. The lady from the motor home came over and introduced herself. She said she and a few extended family members were there for the weekend, to check out the area.

The next morning, we were getting ready to go to church when the lady from the motor home was walking by our campsite. She stopped to chat a minute and asked what we were going to do for the day. We mentioned that we were heading out to church. She replied, "Oh, there are churches around here?" Since we had seen quite a few on the way in, I thought that was a strange comment.

We crossed paths again with the lady from the motor home Sunday evening. She said they had enjoyed the park and would be leaving the next day. Monday morning we headed out to drive a scenic drive. When we returned, we noticed that the motor home was still in the campsite even though it was well past checkout time.

When we walked to the beach we passed by the motor home. The lady saw us and came over. She told us that when they went to leave, the motorhome wouldn't start. One of her family members was calling the motor home manufacturer for advice on what to do.

When we returned from our walk, they gave us an update. They were told the motor home would have to be towed to the nearest city that had a repair facility. They put in a request for a tow and had a rental car dropped off at the campground. An hour later, they received a call from the towing company. The towing company wanted a signed waiver that they would not be responsible for any damage to the motor home caused by hitting trees when they were pulling it out of the campsite.

The lady was getting tears in her eyes as she told us all of this, and she was looking overwhelmed. I got talking to her family member who had called the manufacturer. He and I did some further investigating and determined that a fuse was blown. He found that there were spare fuses in the fuse block. He took a spare, put it in place of the blown fuse, turned the key, and the motor home started up.

Beth let out a whoop and said to the lady, "I was praying that between Steve and your family, they would figure this out."

The lady turned to Beth and in a serious and respectful voice said, "I have heard of your God." Beth then quickly told her what God had done for us. One of her family was already in the driver's seat of the motor home, with the engine running. Beth handed the lady a copy of our story before she got into her motor home. As they were pulling out, the lady had the window down. Looking back at us, she asked, "Where can I learn more about this?"

Beth yelled back. "It's in the Bible!"

So Much Need Out There

Another year when we traveled several hundred miles out of state, we ended up camping in an area with beautiful countryside we could explore. When we came to one crossroad, the view looked as though it had come from a calendar. There was rolling farmland as far as you could see, with small groves of big maple trees in full fall color on nearby ridges. In front of us was a well-kept church with several ancient maples in full color around it. My thought was, *What a great setting for a church. This is where we need to attend a service on Sunday!*

As the week went by, God was impressing on us that we shouldn't go to the church we had seen, but should go to church in town. When we stopped in town we spotted a church building. The sign out front simply stated the name of the church and didn't display the service time. We used the phone book at the campground pay phone to obtain the number for the church, but we were unsuccessful in connecting with anyone. We made another drive into town to see if we could get more information, and we noticed a sign next to the building stating *No parking during church services.* Apparently, the intent was to keep this section of public parking available for church members, but the message on the sign didn't encourage non-members to visit the church.

We spotted another church building as we were driving around. This one's sign out front read *All Welcome* and displayed the service time clearly. My thought was, *Well, it looks as if that's where we'll go to church.*

Sunday morning, we arrived at the church just a few minutes before the service was to start. I took hold of the door handle, opened the door, and looked inside. We saw no one. As we stepped into the foyer a lady appeared and said, "I'm the organist. Come on in. We'll be starting in a couple of minutes."

We went in and sat down. I noticed a couple seated near us. The husband was assisting his wife, who appeared to have health issues. Soon a person went up front. She said, "The pastor is away this week, so we're going to read some passages from the Bible that a hymn is based on, sing some hymns, and have a prayer time."

The service progressed as planned. I thought, *There's not much going on here. If we leave just as soon as this is done, maybe we can make it to the church we saw last week before their service starts.* Before the prayer time, the person leading asked if there were any prayer requests.

The man whose wife appeared to be having medical challenges stood up and said, "I have a request. I love my wife more than ever, but I hate the situation we're in. I know God can heal her, but it doesn't happen." The leader added this concern to the prayer list.

I could identify with having a wife in a situation where you feel hopeless. As the service was closing, I whispered to Beth, "I need to talk to this guy. I'll strike up a conversation with him before he leaves.

Why don't you talk to the person in charge and ask if I can pray with these people?"

After the service Beth went to the front of the sanctuary to ask permission, and I went to the foyer and started talking with the man who had the prayer request. He told me at one point that he had gone to a church that taught about divine healing and had seen some good things happen. I was waiting for Beth to show up. It's not often we are compelled to pray for someone when we are visiting a church. But when it does happen, we believe it is important that the church leadership knows what is taking place and approves.

Beth's head appeared around the side of the wall section separating the foyer from the sanctuary. She said, "It's okay to pray. Go ahead."

I talked awhile more with the man and his wife and prayed with them before they left. A few minutes later, I went to look for Beth and found her and another lady deep in conversation. The lady shared that she had surgery and was well past the point where doctors expected her to have no pain. Yet she was still needing strong pain killers. She had an infection she was dealing with as well. She also said some changes in her life were becoming more difficult to deal with than they should be. She said, "I think it has something to do with spiritual warfare, but I'm not sure."

We sat down facing each other in some fold-up chairs. Beth suggested that the lady tell Satan to stay away from her, in Jesus' name. The lady leaned forward slightly in the chair, with her elbows on her knees and her hands in the air. She closed her eyes and with great conviction said, "Satan, take your hands off me, in Jesus' name!" Immediately, she slumped back in her chair fully relaxed. After about ten seconds she opened her eyes and said, "My pain is gone."

All evidence of infection was completely gone too. The lady looked at us and said, "I'm so glad the leaders didn't close God's house today. And He sent two angels . . ." She looked at us as if to say, *You are angels, aren't you?*

I responded, "We're just two people God has done a lot for, and we share it with people we cross paths with along the way."

After we returned from this trip, I gave Pastor Bill a call and said to him, "The last couple of years, it seems as though every time we travel out of state we meet someone who can benefit from hearing our story. Does God specifically line us up with a particular person, or is there just that much need out there?"

His response was, "Both."

Campsite 20

When our kids were little we would always take vacation in the fall. Beth and I picked up on that pattern again after the kids were on their own. We started scheduling a vacation week and waiting until the last minute to check where fall color would be full and good weather would be predicted for the next week. That was how we determined our general destination. We then would head out and determine where we would stop the first night on the road. From one year to the next, we could end up a thousand miles in the opposite direction from home.

One year when we had been on the road an hour or so, Beth said, "Campsite 20 just came to me." When we arrived at the campground we had selected, we checked out campsite 20. No one was occupying it, but it wasn't suitable for our little trailer. We parked the teardrop elsewhere and spent the next few days walking the local hiking trails and taking in the scenery.

We got to know some of our fellow campers. We chatted with an older couple and mentioned that we had enjoyed the area, but we had hiked all the trails we planned on and now were deciding where else to go next. They suggested we explore one of their favorite areas a couple of hours away. The area had a nice campground and more of the natural features we enjoyed.

The next morning, we drove to the area they had suggested. When we arrived at the campground, only two campsites were available. One was right next to the busy bathhouse, which didn't appeal to us. The other was number 21 at the end of the campground, a short distance from a small stream.

We registered and set up on campsite 21. Quite a few of the

camping rigs around us appeared to belong to people who were out hiking or seeing the scenery. The trailer next to us in campsite 20 seemed deserted. The only sign that someone had been around recently was a checkered tablecloth on the picnic table with a bundle of water bottles on it.

We drove around the area to get the lay of the land. As we were driving we were keeping an eye out for a church to attend the next morning, but we didn't spot any possibilities.

While Beth was showering the next morning, I was puttering around the trailer when a man camped across from us came over and in a local dialect I could barely understand said, "That's the smallest trailer I've ever seen."

I told him the story of how Beth hadn't been well enough to camp and how after God healed her, we bought the little trailer. A lady came out of the trailer next to us, in campsite 20, and walked up to us. She had overheard most of our conversation. We continued the conversation and included her. I said that the trailer attracted interest and stimulated conversation. I shared how we would tell people the story of Beth's healing and also how we acquired the trailer, and the conversation would either shift to talking about God or talking about the trailer.

The lady from campsite 20 said, "Our church is here this weekend for our church camp-out. We're having our church service at the pavilion this morning if you'd like to come."

I went to the bathhouse and yelled into the vent, "Hey, Beth, hurry up! We need to leave for church."

We arrived at the pavilion a few minutes before the service started and met a few people. One of them told us where they were from and the church's denominational background. Somebody let out a whistle and said, "Pastor wants to start the service."

The pastor said, "Come on in and get a seat. I'll set up on the end of the tables." After we found a picnic table to sit at, we watched a few people set up their musical instruments. The pavilion was long and narrow, with picnic tables set end to end the length of the building.

It was a shelter with open sides, and the people attending overflowed to the outside.

The service started with singing a couple of old hymns. The pastor then took prayer requests and updated the congregation on people's needs. He gave details on two deaths and at least another half-dozen people in the congregation who were facing tissues that were lingering and life threatening. He then invited a lady to come up and sing an old-time Gospel song.

When she was finished singing, he said, "If anyone would like to sing a song . . ." he then leaned over a bit and looked down the picnic tables, directly at Beth and me and continued, ". . . or give a testimony, come on up here."

No one went up, but one young man raised his hand. The pastor nodded to him, and the young man broke out singing another old-time Gospel song. While he was singing, the Holy Spirit was prompting me to get up in response to the pastor's request. I was thinking, *Okay, Lord, we're at a meeting of a denomination whose members often believe that the gifts of the Spirit are no longer active. They're facing all this death and big physical challenges, and You want me to get up and talk about getting healed? If You want me to get up, You'll have to give me the words.*

I didn't get much of a direct response from God, yet I just knew I needed to get up. After young man's song ended, I put up my hand. The pastor pointed to me. I said, "Pastor, were you asking for someone to give a testimony?"

His response was, "Come on up here."

I don't remember much about the details of what I said. I recall describing my spinal curvature and leg length issues. I also described how I had viewed God and how I was healed. I do remember saying, "Your congregation is facing a lot of challenges. One thing I've learned is God loves us even when the circumstances make it seem as if He doesn't."

As I was sitting down another song was sung. I said to the older man sitting next to me, "I hope it's okay that I talked about being healed to your church."

He put his hand on my knee and said, "You can talk about what God has done for you at our church anytime. That's what we do at our church."

Beth's Turn

At the end of the song, Beth put up her hand and was asked to get up and give a testimony. Beth had been going through some challenges and was finding that she had to keep focused on what God had done for her. She quickly described her healing and stated that God's truth does not change when our circumstances do. She also talked about never forgetting what God has done for us. She spoke with great conviction.

The pastor's message that day addressed the needs of the congregation. It turned out that the things Beth and I said when we were asked to get up were exactly the things the pastor was planning on pointing out in his message. Once he pointed to me and said, "At one point, he was going around crippled up with a short leg. The Bible says God is a healer. God fixed his leg. It might have taken a while, but God does for us what He says He will do."

We were invited to stay for a potluck after the service. Items were put on the grill, and it would be a while before lunch. We decided to leave so we could get out and drive one of the scenic drives in the area. As we were going to our van, two ladies were walking toward us. One of them was the lady from the trailer on campsite 20. She quietly said, "You're not leaving, are you?" Then she got tears in her eyes and shared with us concerns that were heavy on her heart. Beth gave her a long hug and prayed with her.

The other lady said to Beth, "As soon as you stood up, I knew God had sent you here for her." We stayed for more fellowship and the home cooking.

After lunch, we returned to our campsite. Earlier we had seen a campsite right on the stream that ran through the campground open up just as we left for the church service. I was hoping to move to that site, but it was occupied when we got back. We went for the drive.

It was a beautiful day. We stopped at scenic pullouts and took some short hikes. We had no plans for the evening, so we kept an eye out for some firewood to purchase for a bonfire, but didn't find any.

In the evening there wasn't much going on at our campsite. I suggested to Beth, "Let's check out the rest of the campground."

We walked around the campground, and on a back loop we found the people from the church service. They were along the stream and had a nice bonfire going a few feet away from a long table filled with food. They called us over and said, "Grab some chairs. Do you need something to eat?"

We sat there for quite a while enjoying the river, the bonfire, and the fellowship. I think we were the only people there who weren't wearing a sweatshirt from the local university.

The next morning, several of the church members were packing up their campers. One of the couples who were among the last to leave wandered over and asked us how long we were staying. As they were pulling out, the husband said, "If we don't see you again, we'll see you in heaven." When God is at the center of the interactions, it is remarkable how much of a bond can be developed in one day with people you have never seen before!

21

At the Point of Our Need

OVER THE YEARS, A VARIETY OF THINGS HAVE COME UP WHERE God has opened my eyes to His care, His protection of me, His meeting me at my point of need, and His taking my trauma and injury and remolding me into something new. One incident I recall involves His protection. One winter the price of gasoline was very low. Beth and I decided to save on airfare and drive to Florida for a winter getaway. A few days before we were to return home, we started monitoring weather reports along our anticipated travel route. Spotty tornado activity was predicted in northern Florida, heavy rain in Georgia, and the possibility of severe snowstorms with icy driving conditions in Ohio and Indiana.

Beth was scheduled to work on Saturday. The drive home is usually a two-day drive. Tuesday afternoon we were debating whether to leave Wednesday or enjoy another day and leave Thursday, as originally planned. Tuesday evening we cleaned up the place where we were staying, packed our bags, and put them in the van so we could leave in the morning if we felt it was necessary. We prayed about the situation and decided to check the latest weather reports in the morning.

The morning's weather reports revealed that several tornadoes had passed through the counties to the north of us. Severe weather was predicted for the area we were staying in until midafternoon. Possible snow and icy conditions were still predicted along the route home, but no time frames were pinpointed. We were thinking we would stay put until early afternoon, but then severe weather started passing through. We could see the palm branches whipping in the wind. We decided to shower at the bathhouse by the pool so we wouldn't need to take time to pick up after ourselves inside again. We walked through the wind to the pool. As we reached the bathhouse, I said to Beth, "Let's both pray separately and ask God to show us what to do."

I came back out of the building before she did. The wind gusts had increased. There were big ripples on the surface of the pool. Beth came out and said, "We have to go now!"

"I know," I agreed.

We hurried back to where we were staying, locked up, got in the van, and headed out. We stopped long enough to fill up on gas. While I was filling the gas tank, Beth ran to a Subway restaurant next door and bought two footlong subs. She got in the van, and we drove off into the high winds.

An hour into the drive, it started to rain. The rain became so heavy that traffic slowed to 20 miles an hour. Drivers were keeping five car lengths apart to avoid rear-ending the car ahead. I could only see taillights in front of me half the time. Eventually, cars were pulling off the side of the road. We kept driving. After forty-five minutes of driving in the heavy rain, I said to Beth, "I know we believe God was prompting us to leave immediately, but at the moment it doesn't look as if it was a good idea."

Five minutes after my comment, the rain let up. We had good driving. We drove until early evening and reached a motel in Georgia. Leaving midday committed us to a trip that required two overnight stays on the road instead of only one night. That evening, we looked at discount motel booklets to find a place to stay the next night. I calculated where we should end up in order to have a reasonable drive the next day. We would be at Corbin, Kentucky, near Cumberland Falls State Resort Park. This was the park where we had almost walked off the top of the waterfall after we were first married. We really liked the old Civilian Conservation Corps lodge at the park, but had always felt it was too expensive to stay there. My thought this time around was if we needed lodging anyway, we could pay a bit more and make an old dream come true. We called the lodge, and winter rates were the same as a motel on the highway. We made a reservation.

In the morning, we woke up, got on the road, and continued heading north. Driving conditions were good as we entered the mountains. We were on I-75 in Tennessee, a few miles from the Kentucky border, when Beth spotted a *WATCH FOR FALLEN ROCK* sign. She made the comment, "When I was little and we would drive past a sign like that, I thought we would see a rock fall just like on Wile E. Coyote."

I chuckled and said, "Well, if you'd like, we could park here for a while and wait for one to fall." We both laughed.

On arrival at Cumberland Falls, we checked into the lodge. The lodge only has one room with a view of the river on each floor. We had the river view room on the top floor. We went to see the falls and parked where we had so many years before. In the early evening, Beth and I and one other couple were the only people enjoying the lodge sitting area with the huge fireplace and comfortable rocking chairs.

Weather reports for the route home still showed high potential for snow and icy roads. On our drive north the clouds appeared threatening, but all we ever saw were a few snowflakes. A couple of hundred miles from home it had snowed, but the roads had been cleared. We were still wondering why God had prompted us to leave so urgently. I checked the weather reports again. With our two overnight stays, we had threaded the severe impact of the various weather systems, but it appeared that if we had left later, we would have had the same result.

The next Monday morning when I was at work, another of the supervisors rode up to me on his three-wheeled bike and shouted, "Did you get caught in the rockslide on I-75?"

"What are you talking about?" I asked.

He yelled back, "You know—the rockslide on I-75. You must have. You got home Saturday, didn't you? You must have been right in it!" And he rode off.

I just shrugged my shoulders. I hadn't heard anything about a rockslide. When I got home, I went online. Sure enough, at the exact spot where I had been joking with Beth about seeing a rock fall, there had been a rockslide onto the highway. It was big enough to shut down the interstate for several weeks. Rocks the size of minivans landed in both of the northbound lanes. A huge pine tree was lying on top of them.

People who were at that spot when it happened were trapped, with miles of cars backing up behind them. They were delayed for many hours. Two lanes of 75 mph traffic coming from the south were being rerouted onto a twisty, two-lane road. Police had to coordinate getting the stranded cars and trucks turned around and merged into the oncoming traffic flowing onto the old two-lane route. The rockslide occurred 24 hours after we had passed through!

At Least I'm in the Pool!

About the time I turned fifty, Beth and I started swimming at the local high school pool to stay in shape. This worked well for me because it didn't pound my joints. It also helped the symmetry of the muscles in my torso. I did notice that my swimming pace was slow compared to other lap swimmers, but I was swimming to stay in shape, not getting ready to compete in an athletic event.

At one point, a new swimmer showed up. We talked once in a while and got to know each other. Eventually, he told me he had set a school record as a swimmer in high school and his times were good enough that he was invited to a swim camp for Olympic hopefuls. Despite adhering to a training schedule that consisted of swimming most of the day, he didn't achieve the level of performance of the most elite swimmers.

When he told me that story, my mind went back to watching the 1972 Olympics decades earlier. His story brought to mind the fact that it wasn't easy to make the Olympic team as a swimmer just because you had a normal body and long arms. I shared my medical history with him. I had my swimsuit on, so my scar line was visible. I also shared with him the story of how God had straightened out my spine.

Then I said, "I might not swim as fast as some people, but at least I'm in the pool!"

He stared at me and said, "That makes me think I should ask God what else He has for me!" His response showed me that he considered what I had experienced to be far more valuable than a high school swimming record.

I was starting to fully realize that too.

The Tonka Truck

Even taking a simple interest in a hobby has shown me what God has done for me. When I was in my late fifties, I dug out some of my old toys. I found the 1958 Tonka truck I had inherited from the neighbors more than fifty years earlier. It was in a few pieces and some parts were missing. The truck was originally dark blue from the factory, but most of the paint had been worn off by the time I was given it. My mom had repainted it the same light green and beige colors as my dad's Forman truck. When I was in junior high, I repainted it orange and white for some reason.

I recently had become interested in old Tonka trucks and had some interactions with a local person who had restored several of these. I told him the history of my truck and asked, "Should I restore it to make it like new, repainting it the factory color?"

He said, "I would restore it to the way you remember it."

I took his advice, smoothing out some paint chips and doing some bodywork on a bent fender. I cleaned spots of old paint off the tires and ordered some replacement parts. I found paint matching the green and beige colors my mom had painted it in the 1960s. It felt strange to take a beautiful, shiny new replacement grill and rough it up so paint would stick.

As I was going through the process, it was as though God was showing me that the process was similar to what He had done for me. He had smoothed out all the effects of the emotional, spiritual, and physical trauma I had experienced throughout my life and was forming me into what I needed to be—complete and unique. When the Tonka truck was finished, it was complete and unique too. The local Tonka community thought it was spectacular.

No Generational Aftereffects

In the growth of our children, Beth and I have witnessed the unfolding of the twenty to thirty years one medical journal estimated it would take to see if the children of Wilms survivors would be affected by a parent's radiation treatments. Our children have had no aftereffects.

We also have been blessed with several grandchildren who show no aftereffects. It seems that when each one is born, it becomes a time for everyone in the family to reflect on our blessings. After our first grandchild was born, the extended family got together after his dedication at church. He had all eight of his great-grandparents at the gathering. My dad commented that it must be nice to be that little and have that many people love you.

When it is my turn to hold a new grandchild within a day after he or she is born, I think about what it must have been like for me as a newborn. They are so small and helpless. At that age, I had gone through the trauma of not breathing and having the bruised abdomen. As we see the grandkids from time to time as the weeks go by and they grow, I reflect on what stage I was in with my medical treatment at their age.

We had a family gathering once when one of our grandchildren was about four weeks old. She was having problems with trapping some air after she took in nutrition, which caused gas pains in her tiny digestive tract. She sounded so miserable that it made me wonder what gives children of that age the will to live when their current pain totally fills their world. I realized that at that age, I had been recovering from major surgery and was on the special pain medication.

I walked through the house with my new granddaughter on my shoulder and patted her back. She started to settle down. This experience made me realize that until I was several months old, most of my infant life I had experienced the severe pain involved with recovering from two surgeries and the radiation treatments. Just my having the will to live had to have been provided by God's hand.

At the Point of Dad's Need

Perhaps one of the most dramatic examples I have seen of God meeting a person at his or her point of need involves my father in his last days. When I was in high school, Dad had a heart attack. He had a second one just after he turned sixty. This resulted in quintuple bypass surgery. In his later years, his heart would not fire properly and he would become fatigued. He was also diagnosed with Parkinson's disease, so his right hand would shake.

Eventually, Dad quit driving and was slowly losing the ability to care for himself. He and Mom moved into an assisted living facility. Dad went there with the intention of rehabilitating himself and returning home. One day when I was visiting, I pushed him in a wheelchair from the dining hall back to their room. He rang the call bell to have an aid transfer him from the wheelchair to his chair. I had to leave, so I stood behind him and gave him a hug. All of a sudden, it felt as if I were four years old again, riding on his shoulders while he was running through the living room in their first house. It was a wonderful childhood memory, but on the way home I was grieving the fact that he was no longer what he used to be.

One evening at home, the Holy Spirit impressed on me that something significant was going to happen on June 30. I didn't have any indication what it would be related to. June 30 came and went, with nothing notable that I knew of taking place. In early July I was visiting my parents and Dad was asleep, so I was talking with Mom in the next room. She said, "The other day, your dad was sitting on the edge of the bed and said, 'God, You're going to have to help me. I can't do this on my own anymore.'"

"What day did that happen?" I asked her.

"It was the last day of June," she replied.

The time came when Dad wanted to return home from the assisted living facility. Mom arranged for in-home care, and Dad enjoyed a few good days back at home. He was able to get around the yard with his walker and sit on the deck. Then his physical condition deteriorated further. He would get confused from time to time. He could also get quite agitated. A few weeks before he passed away, Dad asked us how we would do if he were not around. It became evident that he still felt responsible for the family.

My brother was a manager at the road construction company Dad had worked for most of his working life. From time to time over the years, he would pick Dad up and show him one of their new jobs. Dad would volunteer advice on how he thought things should be done. Dad said to my brother, "I'm the most worried about you. Who will be there to get you out of a jam if I'm not around?"

My brother lovingly replied, "I'm fifty years old and you taught me everything you know. I'll be all right."

After this interaction, Dad accepted hospice care. One Sunday evening, we visited and Dad was in bed asleep. The next day, I got a text from Mom. It said, "I thought we were going to lose Dad last night."

I called her and she said right after we had left, his heart had started skipping beats and then started beating only once a minute. This went on for several hours. Eventually, his heart slowly started to beat more frequently, until it returned to normal. In the morning, Mom called hospice and they told her that what she described simply doesn't happen.

One evening two weeks later, the same thing happened. This time Dad went as long as three minutes between heartbeats, and his body got cold. After a few hours, Mom called hospice and they sent a nurse out. The nurse checked Dad's oxygen saturation level, and it was normal! She told Mom, "We can't declare him dead when he has a normal oxygen saturation level." Then she left.

As morning neared, Dad's heart started beating more regularly. Midmorning he actually opened his eyes and looked out the window. He turned to Mom and in a joyful tone said, "I died last night."

At this point, he was capable of saying just a couple of words at a time. We were surprised that he could say a complete sentence. After that experience, Mom didn't have to give Dad any more medication to control his agitation. His right hand was no longer shaking either.

The next Saturday, I was at the house. Mom had the head of Dad's bed tilted up, and his line of sight was at the top of the wall beyond the bed. He was looking at the spot intently and moving his eyes from side to side. It appeared that he was reliving what he had experienced when his heart was barely beating.

From time to time, he would glance at me and make a comment. At one point, he said, "Heaven." Then he looked back at the wall, glanced back to me, and said, "Halfway up." Looking at the wall again, he suddenly started moving both arms with great strength and perfect control, as though he were directing a choir.

Four days later, Dad died. The in-home care person who was with Mom and Dad when he passed said she had helped people at the end of their lives for years and had never seen anyone pass away as peacefully as Dad.

A few days after Dad's funeral, I stopped by a monument company to see what they had available for headstones. The person who met me at the door extended the usual condolences. I felt I should let him know that I was doing all right. I told him the story of Dad's last days and how seeing God's hand reach out to Dad made a big difference in how his passing affected me. The monument salesperson said, "My dad passed away, it didn't go so well for him. Hearing you tell your story really helps."

For me, witnessing what God had done for Dad in his last days made all the difference in dealing with his passing. It was obvious that God was reaching out to Dad in a special way after Dad told Him he couldn't do it on his own anymore. In fact, it seems I had already gone through my time of grieving on the way home from the care facility, the evening that I had hugged him and had remembered the way he carried me on his shoulders when I was little. Reaching out to Dad the way He had was also one of God's biggest gifts to me.

22

Followed by Goodness and Mercy

OVER THE YEARS FOLLOWING MY INITIAL HEALING, TWO SITUAtions came up where I was experiencing new physical traumas. God's solution was to work more miracles as part of the healing process. Prior to my spine being straightened, I had developed an interest in recumbent bikes. The motivating factor was being able to pedal without having my pelvis rock up and down, which caused me musculoskeletal pain afterward. At one point, I had built a homemade recumbent bike from an old girl's 20-inch bike and a chopped up ten speed. This bike sat in the yard barn for many years after I started riding regular bikes again.

One evening I said to Beth, "Let's go for a bike ride. I'm going to get out the homemade recumbent." We took a good ride. When we came back into the yard, I was going a little fast. I coasted into the backyard to lose some speed because getting off this bike was tricky. The front wheel hit a lump of dirt and twisted. I was unable to break my fall as I fell to my right side. When my shoulder hit the ground, I could hear a crunching sound and the nerves in my shoulder lit up.

Beth and I prayed over my injury and went to the med center, where they took X-rays. With the sound and what I felt when it happened, I was fully expecting to hear that I had shattered my shoulder. It turned out that I had fractured my scapula. The doctor at the med center said, "You're going to be really sore tomorrow!"

The next day, I certainly could still feel the effect of what had happened, but the level of pain he predicted did not occur. I was sent to an orthopedic doctor, who reviewed my X-rays. He told me I had rotator cuff damage that was historical and not related to the fall. He said they could do an MRI and possible surgery. He then pulled his shirt collar down a bit and showed me a scar line where he had gone through the same surgery. Then he said, "But it doesn't necessarily help much."

This orthopedic doctor decided to give me an elastic rubber strip to use in an exercise program that would strengthen my shoulder as it healed. I was also told that the crunching sound I had heard when I fell was my tendons rolling. He told me once this happens the tendons want to remain in the new position, so after the shoulder healed I would be left with arthritic-type symptoms.

The back of my shoulder felt as if it had a separation in it. Beth and I would pray over it every day. Beth also had to drive me to work because I simply couldn't move the stick shift on my car. This didn't take much force to do, and it wasn't a matter of pain. I simply couldn't move my arm at that particular angle even for the short distance moving the shift stick required.

I started having Beth pray over my arms three times a day in the same manner as Pastor Bill. My right shoulder would move when she prayed. It would move back, it would warm up, it would extend forward, and it would warm up again. The shoulder would then go back to its original position, and the soreness would be greatly reduced.

On my next visit to the doctor, I wasn't feeling very healed. Yet he reviewed my latest X-rays and said, "You're healing up like gangbusters!" He told me I would need physical therapy after a few more weeks of healing.

Beth and I continued praying, and I continued the exercises. On my next doctor visit, I was still feeling sore and still didn't feel healed. More X-rays were taken. The doctor reviewed them with me. "Here is your scapula," he said. "When you fracture your scapula, bone growth occurs on the edge of it as part of the healing process. What we watch for is the bone growing into your shoulder joint. Look at that line of new bone! It trails off, going into the joint. Even your rotator cuff damage from the past is almost gone! That's just beautiful!"

Normally, my type of injury required a one-year follow-up to ensure that the joint wasn't compromised by new bone growth. But the doctor said I was ready for physical therapy, and I wouldn't be required to follow up with him.

Physical therapy was supposed to be a seven-week process. I was still tender at my first visit. The physical therapist put his hand on the left side of my back. He asked, "Can you reach behind your back and touch my hand?" I was able to do this, but the muscles it involved were very tender. Then he held his hand in front of me and had me push on his hand from a couple of different angles. Then he asked me an odd question: "Why are you here?"

I replied, "Because the doctor sent me."

"Well, you don't need to come back," was his response. He gave me a stronger elastic band and told me to continue the exercises until my shoulder felt normal in day-to-day activities.

After a few more weeks of praying over the shoulder and doing the exercises, I was pretty much back to normal. I now have virtually none of the arthritic symptoms predicted by the doctor. I still have Beth pray for me in the same manner from time to time if I am feeling a little stiff in my shoulders or my legs.

Snow Fracture

A second incident happened a couple of years later. The snow at the end of our driveway was encroaching on where we would drive. I bought a new pair of gloves and a shiny new ice spud. I put on the gloves, grabbed the spud, and went outside to chop the icy mounds of snow into chunks so I could move them out of the way. Things went well until I felt a sharp pain in my right hand, below the base of my pinky. My new gloves weren't very flexible, and the bulky pinky finger had wedged itself on the top of the ice spud's handle. When the rest of my glove slid down the shiny new handle, my pinky bent outward.

I had Beth pray over my hand. That night, I put my hand in a big old sock, with the end rolled in a ball. I grasped this ball to support my hand as I went to sleep. In the morning, the pain hadn't improved. I bought an inexpensive hand brace at the drug store, put it on, and went to work. That night I slept with my hand in the sock again.

In the morning again there was no improvement, but there was still pain. Beth and I decided that I needed to go to urgent care. We prayed over my hand again before we left. As we prayed, I could feel the bone in my hand moving. I could feel a grinding sensation, and Beth and I both could hear a snapping, popping sound.

At urgent care they took X-rays, and the doctor informed me of the results: "You have a spiral fracture. These are usually difficult to set correctly. Yours is perfectly lined up. Don't flex your hand, and go directly to the physical therapy office to have a molded splint made."

I was then sent to an orthopedic doctor, who monitored my progress. I was instructed that I could take my hand out of the splint to wash it, but I was not to flex it. I was told that the healing process would take three weeks, and my hand would need physical therapy afterward due to weakened muscles, since I would not be using them during healing. My follow-up appointment was scheduled for nearly four weeks after the incident.

After three weeks, when I had my hand out of the splint to wash it I put my elbow on the table with my hand up in the air. I said to God, *I was told I would heal in three weeks, but I'm not going to move my hand on my own until I have an X-ray. So if You want it to move, You will have to move it.* The fingers on my hand started to move slowly forward to a position similar to grasping a tennis ball and then curved toward the base of my hand. Next, the fingers went back to their original position and then flexed backward to a degree. I went to God in this way twice a day, until my appointment. The range of motion would increase a bit each day.

At the next doctor appointment, my bone was declared healed and I was sent to physical therapy. When my range of motion was measured, the therapist showed me the measuring gauge and said, "See how far you are able to move your fingers? That is farther than expected for recovering from your type of injury." She then said,

"Here are the exercises I want you to do." She handed me a printout of exercises describing moving my fingers foreword in a motion similar to grasping a tennis ball. The next exercise took the fingers from this position and rolled them toward the base of the hand. A third exercise was flexing the fingers slightly backward. These were the very same motions my hand had gone through after I had prayed! Due to the "head start" God had given me on the physical therapy, I was able to skip part of the sessions and was released from medical attention earlier than expected.

Getting a Miracle?

From time to time I have heard comments concerning my story, such as "It was sure nice God did that for you. He doesn't do that for everyone." Or, "God did miracles for you. How do I get my miracle?" When a person asks me these types of questions, he or she typically has a specific health issue in mind. How to get a miracle is an interesting question. The 1975 edition of *The Random House College Dictionary* I used back in my college days defines a *miracle* as "an event in the physical world that surpasses all known human or natural powers and is ascribed to a divine or supernatural cause."

    I would point out that according to this dictionary definition, we all have had miracles that got us where we are. First of all, the earth was created by a miracle—the result of God speaking it into existence: "In the beginning God created the heavens and the earth" (Genesis 1:1 NKJV).

    How God knits each person together in his or her mother's womb is something scientists don't fully understand. It's a miraculous process all by itself. Psalm 100:3 (NKJV) says, "Know that the Lord, He is God; it is He who has made us, and not we ourselves; we are His people and the sheep of His pasture."

    The fact that God loved humanity enough to send Jesus to defeat Satan and give us eternal life (if we believe on Him) is also, by dictionary definition, a miracle since it has a supernatural cause. "For God so loved the world that He gave His only begotten Son, that whoever believes in Him should not perish but have everlasting life" (John 3:16 NKJV).

In my case, when I was born I had a specific issue that needed a miracle. Looking back, I did nothing at all to get the miracle of surviving my first months. A newborn doesn't have an intellectual understanding of health, illness, or even God in the sense that an adult can contemplate and react to a situation on these terms. At the time I was a newborn, as far as human intellectual/physical/spiritual concern surrounding me, it was my parents who bore the burden of struggling with the situation.

The Old Testament book of Zechariah, chapter 12, verse 10 (NKJV) says, "And I will pour on the house of David and on the inhabitants of Jerusalem the Spirit of grace and supplication; then they will look on Me whom they pierced." I believe my mother was given the Spirit of grace and supplication when she was dealing with the life-threatening appendix issue she experienced at nine years old. She learned to turn to God to bring her through, and she developed a trusting faith. These things enabled her to keep going from day to day, facing what appeared impossible to overcome, yet bringing her cares to God and trusting that He would work it all out for the ultimate good. When my situation had to be dealt with, Mom took the same approach. Along with that, Dad's willingness to do whatever it took to help me as a newborn, and his pushing the doctors to do something, illustrate how we must be willing to act when God calls us to do so.

When I was in my preschool and elementary school years, I had a healthy view of God. I believe I was living under the umbrella of the Spirit of grace and supplication over my parents. In my junior high years, I started filtering my view of God through my experiences. The thoughts I would have about not measuring up to the standards of the world began to erode my view of God. My personal spirit of grace and supplication was not developing. My focus shifted to how I appeared shortchanged compared to my peers, and from there I moved to trying to figure out why God had let that happen to me.

John 10:10 (NKJV) says, "The thief does not come except to steal, and to kill, and to destroy." Satan was taking advantage of the fact that my thoughts were leading me into a state of mind where I was losing the grace to deal properly with the challenges I faced, because I wasn't going to God with my concerns. As life went on, my skewed viewpoint became more entrenched. I believe that had I put into actual practice the principles Beth and I were presented with in our wedding meditation, life would have gone much smoother. I would have adopted a more proper view of God, and I would have been able to rest in His peace along the way as challenges came up.

The miracles I experienced when I was forty-four happened without really going to God in advance. In fact, I didn't show up at the first healing service for myself. I took Beth, knowing only God could heal her. God certainly responded with a miracle for me. I believe in my case, the timing of this was meant to draw me to Him.

Despite how I had slipped in my view of God, He was always there watching over me and protecting me. The mustard seed of faith planted in my early years may have been dormant, but it was still there. It was enough to turn me to God when Beth needed healing, and it was waiting to take root after my initial healing. The biggest thing I had to come to realize, in order to allow that seed to grow, was that sickness, disease, and disability weren't in God's original plan. They exist because Adam and Eve were enticed with the devil's temptation and turned their focus away from what God had told them. I had to come to understand that God loves me and was drawing me to Him.

Over the many years since that first healing service, I have had the usual challenges many people face come up in my life. I believe that God has provided doctors, and that He often uses their skills and knowledge to meet my needs. At the same time, if I need a deep sliver removed, I go to God with my concern as I am on the way to the doctor, and I recognize that it is God who created my body to heal itself. I ask Him to watch over the procedure and the healing process.

I also have had some lingering challenges from my early medical history, such as fatigue and occasional tightness in the muscles along my scar line that are not in a normal orientation. Sometimes these symptoms resurface, even though God has straightened out my spine and much of the scar tissue tension has gone away. I have learned to go to Him as they come up, and He walks me through each one of these challenges.

As I shared with you in the stories about my scar tissue loosening, my shoulder injury healing so well, and my hand injury doing the same, I have had additional miracles take place. Most of them have been unexpected or have taken place with a timing I wouldn't have chosen myself. For some challenges that have come up, I thought I needed another immediate miracle but didn't receive one. In those instances, God took care of me in other ways.

Approaching God with Needs

Perhaps the question should not be "How do I get my miracle?" but rather, "How do I get what I need from God?" Over the years, I have learned several things that I believe relate to my walk with God and how I should approach Him with my needs. Here is a summary of the key points I have learned (all Scriptures in this list are taken from the NKJV):

> God loves me and did not preplan problems for me. "He does not afflict willingly, nor grieve the children of men" (Lamentations 3:33).

> God wants what is best for me. "Every good gift and every perfect gift is from above, and comes down from the Father of lights, with whom there is no variation or shadow of turning" (James 1:17).

> Satan comes to steal, kill, and destroy (see John 10:10). But Jesus came to destroy Satan's works: "For this purpose the Son of God was manifested, that He might destroy the works of the devil" (1 John 3:8).

> What I see with my eyes is not necessarily what is the true reality. What God's Word says about my situation is the true reality. I need faith to believe what God's Word says. "Faith is the substance

of things hoped for, the evidence of things not seen" (Hebrews 11:1).

What I think is best for me may not be what God knows is best for me. "He knows our frame; He remembers that we are dust" (Psalm 103:14). I need to have faith that as I seek God when I don't understand what's happening, He is doing what is best for me. I can't presume that He has to work things out the way I think best.

When I humble myself and bring my concerns to God, He responds. This includes admitting it when I have strayed from Him and have created my own problems. In other words, it includes repenting for missing the mark. "Humble yourselves in the sight of the Lord, and He will lift you up" (James 4:10).

When I come to God with a need that doctors have no answer for, He may respond in a number of different ways. He may respond with an immediate miracle, exactly as I would like. He may respond with a miracle that seems delayed to me. He may respond by healing me slowly, over time. (By dictionary definition, being *divinely* healed over time is a miracle.) Or He may give me the grace to deal with the situation as it is and give me His peace. "My grace is sufficient for you, for My strength is made perfect in weakness" (2 Corinthians 12:9). For years, that last verse seemed to me as if it simply didn't fit with other Bible texts that describe God as a loving healer. When I was reflecting on this, I realized that it is God giving sufficient grace, which surpasses all known human or natural powers. Therefore, by dictionary definition, this gift of grace also is a miracle.

There can be things going on in the spirit world that I do not know. If that is the case, God will turn the spiritual challenges to my good. (For a good example, see the end of the book of Job.) Romans 8:28 tells us, "We know that all things work together for good to those who love God, to those who are the called according to His purpose."

In most situations, God wants me to take action after I have brought my concerns to Him. "As the body without the spirit is dead, so faith without works is dead also" (James 2:26). One of the actions I'm called to take is speaking the truth related to my situation from God's Word. God may direct me to speak to a mountain of sickness or disease. Jesus said, "If you have faith as a mustard seed, you will say to this mountain, 'Move from here to there,' and it will move" (Matthew 17:20). The action may be binding and breaking the power of an evil spirit in Jesus' name, or speaking healing in Jesus' name: "He gave them power over unclean spirits, to cast them out, and to heal all kinds of sickness and all kinds of disease" (Matthew 10:1).

How do I know what God wants me to do in a particular situation? I believe there are several ways God leads. God and His Word are one, and God performs His Word. Going to His Word for guidance is going to Him. When I was three years old, I was given a bookmark that illustrated this. It had statements printed on it with corresponding biblical texts, statements such as, *If you are mourning, read Matthew 5:4. If you are afraid, read Deuteronomy 31:8. If you are happy, read Philippians 4:4.* God also gives us the gifts of the Spirit to enable us to walk through difficult situations. For example, the Bible teaches that praying in the Spirit edifies us (see 1 Corinthians 14:4). If we are seeking to draw closer to God, the ancient practice of fasting to focus on Him may be something we are prompted to do (see Matthew 6:16–18). James 4:6–7 states a simple way that we can line up with what God wants for us: "'God resists the proud, but gives grace to the humble.' Therefore submit to God. Resist the devil and he will flee from you." After bringing my concern to God and doing what He directs me to do, I need to rest in Him with trusting faith.

As I look back on my family history, every time challenges came up that were beyond human control, and the people involved recognized that God was the only answer and humbly gave the situation to Him, He came through for them one way or another.

I believe I really need to get on my knees and give things to God, trusting that through His Spirit He will walk me through each situation with what is ultimately for my good in mind. I believe I need to read what God's Word says about the situations that come up and take my concerns to Him. I then need to take action as the Bible prescribes for the situation I am facing. After doing what I can, I need to trust and rest in Him.

Trusting and Transformed

I have learned these truths well, but it can be a challenge to keep practicing them consistently as the speed bumps and potholes of life in a fallen world come up. I can tend to slip back into old ways of thinking and old habits.

The Bible speaks of being transformed by the renewing of your mind. My experience is that the renewing of my mind with biblical truth needs to be a continuous thing to prevent me from slipping back into old behavior patterns and ways of thinking. To deal with this, I need to daily do what Proverbs 3:5–6 (NKJV) says:

> Trust in the Lord with all your heart,
> And lean not on your own understanding;
> In all your ways acknowledge Him,
> And He shall direct your paths.

Even with all the ups and downs I have experienced, I can truly summarize my life by paraphrasing Psalm 23:6 this way: "Surely the goodness and mercy of God the Father, Jesus the Son, and the Holy Spirit have followed me all the days of my life."

My prayer is that as you have read the account of my life, you have been able to reflect on your own life and see where God has been reaching out to you with His goodness and mercy. If you have not accepted Jesus as your Savior, I invite you to do so. Romans 10:9–10 (NIV) tells you how: "If you declare with your mouth, "Jesus is Lord," and believe in your heart that God raised him from the dead, you will be saved. For it is with your heart that you believe and are justified, and it is with your mouth that you profess your faith and are saved."

Because in the end, you and I can't stand on our own. When we invite God into our lives, however, He will do more than we can ever ask or imagine.

Acknowledgments

The authors would like to recognize the following libraries and their staff for the invaluable assistance they provided throughout our investigation of historical medical information:

- A. Alfred Taubman Health Sciences Library-University of Michigan
- Clarke Historical Library-Central Michigan University
- Grand Rapids Public Library
- Grand Valley State University Libraries (Allendale and Pew Campuses)
- Library of Michigan (Lansing, Michigan)
- Michigan State University Library
- Spectrum Health Sciences Library (Grand Rapids, Michigan)
- Toronto Public Library
- Western University Library (London, Canada)

The authors would also like to acknowledge the following individuals for their invaluable help in various ways throughout our writing process:

- Dr. Jerry Battista, Ph.D., retired medical physicist of the London Regional Cancer Program, London Health Sciences Centre, and Professor Emeritus, Departments of Medical Biophysics and Oncology, Western University, London, Canada.
- Dr. Thomas Brink, M.D.
- Winnifred Poll (Steve's mother), who provided several artifacts and records, as well as sharing her recollection of the events surrounding Steve's medical history.
- Trish Konieczny, writing consultant, for her help in preparing this book for publication. Her technical editing skills and encouragement to see things from the readers' viewpoint have been key to us completing this book in its current form.

About the Authors

Steve and Beth Poll have been married since 1983. Steve's career has been in the food industry, in the area of quality supervision. Beth has dealt with issues ranging from HIV to COVID-19 throughout her career as a hospital-based bedside RN. They have three grown children and a growing number of grandchildren.

Both Steve and Beth continue to volunteer at a healing ministry. With all God has done for them in the area of healing, they want to pass on the vision they have of the help and wholeness God offers to every person in need of His touch.

For recreation, Steve and Beth enjoy Lake Michigan and its beaches. They even took surfing lessons on Lake Michigan on a day when there were three-foot to five-foot waves! They also enjoy bike riding and lap swimming to keep physically fit. For several years, they have treated lap swimming as a hobby, swimming in the pools at various major universities they pass by when they are traveling. They haven't recently run into any bears that are after their backpacks!